Twelfth Night

WILLIAM SHAKESPEARE

Oxford Literature Companions

Series consultant: Peter Buckroyd

OXFORD

UNIVERSITY PRESS

Contents

Themes · 74

Love · 74
Desire and sexuality · 77
Deception · 79
Madness and wisdom · 80
Cruelty and death · 82

Performance · 84

Performance history · 84
Metatheatricality · 86
Performance as a reading · 86
Concepts underpinning performance · 89
Performing character · 91
Performing gender and sexuality · 92
Film versions of the play · 93

Critical Views · 94

Reading approaches · 94
Beginning to apply critical views · 96
Interpreting character · 98
Interpreting comedy · 98
Interpreting narrative · 100
Interpreting endings · 101
Developing your own readings · 103

Skills and Practice · 104

Exam skills · 104
Planning and structuring an answer · 107
Sample questions · 110
Sample answers · 111
Writing about extracts · 114

Glossary · 118

Introduction

What are Oxford Literature Companions?

Oxford Literature Companions is a series designed to provide you with comprehensive support for popular set texts. You can use the Companion alongside your play, using relevant sections during your studies or using the book as a whole for revision.

Each Companion includes detailed guidance and practical activities on:

- **Plot and Structure**
- **Context**
- **Genre**
- **Characterization and Roles**
- **Language**
- **Themes**
- **Performance**
- **Critical Views**
- **Skills and Practice**

How does this book help with exam preparation?

As well as providing guidance on key areas of the play, throughout this book you will also find 'Upgrade' features. These are tips to help with your exam preparation and performance.

In addition, in the extensive **Skills and Practice** chapter, the 'Exam skills' section provides detailed guidance on areas such as how to prepare for the exam, understanding the question, planning your response and hints for what to do (or not do) in the exam.

In the **Skills and Practice** chapter there is also a bank of **Sample questions** and **Sample answers**. The **Sample answers** are marked and include annotations and a summative comment.

How does this book help with terminology?

Throughout the book, key terms are **highlighted** in the text and explained on the same page. There is also a detailed **Glossary** at the end of the book that explains, in the context of the play, all the relevant literary terms highlighted in this book.

Which edition of the play has this book used?

Quotations and character names have been taken from the Oxford School Shakespeare edition of *Twelfth Night* (ISBN 978-019-832871-1)

How does this book work?

Each book in the Oxford Literature Companions series follows the same approach and includes the following features:

- **Key quotations** from the play
- **Key terms** explained on the page and linked to a complete glossary at the end of the book
- **Activity boxes** to help improve your understanding of the text
- **Upgrade** tips to help prepare you for your assessment

Activity boxes to help improve your understanding of the play

Key quotations from the play

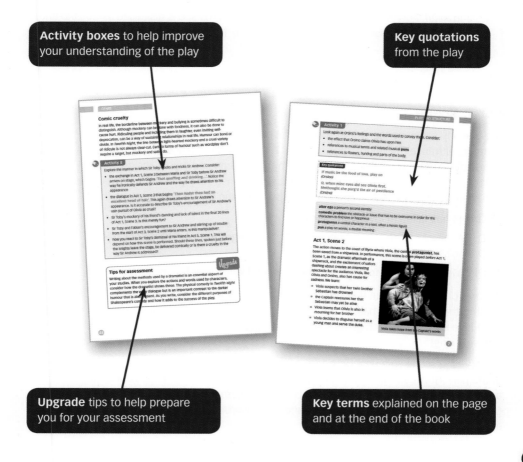

Upgrade tips to help prepare you for your assessment

Key terms explained on the page and at the end of the book

Studying drama

Drama is a special type of text. Unlike a prose novel, where a narrator offers you a way to understand characters and events, drama relies on performance to reveal feelings and motivation. Drama shows, rather than tells.

Although you will probably be reading *Twelfth Night* 'on the page', try to view a performance on stage or in film in order to appreciate fully the dramatic effect of the play. You should be aware that different directors will choose to have the play performed in different ways. Each version of the play offers a reading of the text – a director's interpretation of the way lines are delivered, facial expression, movement, costume, setting, staging and timing.

As you study *Twelfth Night*, take note of the events of the play, but also the way the drama is structured. Consider when characters enter and exit the stage, who speaks, who is silent and what the audience – and the characters – do *and* don't know at various points.

Note: In the body of this book, Viola is always referred to by her name, rather than 'Cesario'. Bear in mind, however, that from Act 1, Scene 4 onwards she is disguised as Cesario and, even when her disguise is revealed in Act 5, Scene 1, she remains dressed as her **alter ego**.

Plot

Act 1, Scene 1

The opening scene concerns the sorrow of a powerful man. It begins with the dramatic entrance of Orsino, Duke of Illyria. The scene takes place in his palace and, as he enters the stage, he is accompanied by attendants and music. His opening speech is melancholic. He addresses the musicians, instructing them to play but then tells them to stop. Orsino, it appears, is despondent and the audience learns that:

- Orsino has fallen in love with Olivia, a countess
- Olivia refuses to see Valentine, Orsino's messenger, and she therefore rejects Orsino's entreaties of love
- Olivia is in mourning for her dead brother, and will grieve for seven years.

Orsino's parting speech in this scene suggests that Olivia's love for him would outstrip the feelings she has for her dead brother, claiming that she'll understand what love is once the **'rich golden shaft'** has **'fill'd / Her sweet perfections with one self king!'**

The opening scene sets up a **comedic problem**, which is resolved during the course of the play: How can these two characters find happiness? To some audiences, it appears that Olivia's grief is excessive. Likewise, whether Orsino is truly in love with Olivia or whether he is simply lovesick and self-absorbed, is a debate you might explore as you study the play.

Activity 1

Look again at Orsino's feelings and the words used to convey them. Consider:

- the effect that Orsino claims Olivia has upon him
- references to musical terms and related musical **puns**
- references to flowers, hunting and parts of the body.

Key quotations

If music be the food of love, play on
(Orsino)

**O, when mine eyes did see Olivia first,
Methought she purg'd the air of pestilence**
(Orsino)

---

alter ego a person's second identity

comedic problem the obstacle or issue that has to be overcome in order for the characters to find love or happiness

protagonist a central character in a text, often a heroic figure

pun a play on words; a double meaning

Act 1, Scene 2

The action moves to the coast of Illyria where Viola, the central **protagonist**, has been saved from a shipwreck. In performance, this scene is often played *before* Act 1, Scene 1, as the dramatic aftermath of a shipwreck, and the excitement of sailors dashing about creates an interesting spectacle for the audience. Viola, like Olivia and Orsino, also has cause for sadness. We learn:

- Viola suspects that her twin brother Sebastian has drowned
- the Captain reassures her that Sebastian may yet be alive
- Viola learns that Olivia is also in mourning for her brother
- Viola decides to disguise herself as a young man and serve the duke.

Viola takes hope from the Captain's words

The inclusion of suffering and death in the first two scenes of the play seems at odds with the usually light feel of a comedy, but this scene introduces elements that will lead to a happy **resolution**. The possibility that Sebastian is alive and his likeness to Viola provide a route to untangling problems.

Viola's resourcefulness – her ability to find a solution to her problems – is shown here, and provides a contrast to the moping melancholy of the duke and countess. It suggests that Viola has the power to make her own happiness. Viola's adoption of disguise is crucial to some of the misunderstandings that occur later, but it also helps the characters discover love in the end.

bawdy humour jokes based on sex and risqué matters

physical comedy where humour arises from movement and manner

resolution the part of a story where problems are overcome and order is restored

Act 1, Scene 3

A third setting – Olivia's house – is introduced now, along with characters who are more recognizably comic. Sir Toby Belch, Olivia's pleasure-seeking uncle, resides there, and his drinking companion Sir Andrew Aguecheek is temporarily staying. Maria, Olivia's lady-in-waiting, attempts to keep them in check.

- Maria warns Sir Toby to control his excessive habits – and those of Sir Andrew.
- Sir Toby half-jokingly defends Sir Andrew, praising his supposed talents.
- Sir Andrew arrives and confirms his own foolishness.
- Maria leaves the two men to converse. Sir Andrew dances as they exit.

Sir Toby appears to be a sort of rebellious figure; an overgrown schoolboy. Part of the comedy in this scene results from the excessive drinking of a man whose behaviour should be more proper. There is something comic about his drunken antics and partying while his niece grieves, and something disrespectful too.

Sir Andrew is often the butt of Sir Toby's jesting. It emerges that he encourages Sir Andrew to woo Olivia, in spite of the unlikelihood of the pairing. Sir Andrew's ability to fund their nightly drinking also seems to appeal to Sir Toby. The misunderstandings, **bawdy humour** and dancing give a lightness to this scene. On stage, Sir Toby is normally presented as overweight and Sir Andrew as thin and weak, echoing the classic comic double act. The wayward knights' drunken antics give actors much scope for **physical comedy**.

Key quotations

I am sure care's an enemy to life.
(Sir Toby)

I am a fellow o' th' strangest mind i' th' world
(Sir Andrew)

Activity 2

Different types of humour are used in Act 1, Scene 3. Make a list of the humorous moments and lines. You don't need to apply specific terms for types of humour yet, but try to explain why these moments are funny.

You could use a table like the one below to record your notes.

Quotation	Analysis
Maria: Ay, but you must confine yourself within the modest limits of order. Sir Toby: Confine? I'll confine myself no finer than I am. These clothes are good enough to drink in... (Act 1, Scene 3)	Sir Toby takes Maria's use of the word 'confine' and plays with it, using it in a different sense. It's also funny because of his blatant disregard for decency and her advice.

Act 1, Scene 4

This scene takes us forward in time slightly. Viola, in disguise as Cesario, has been in service to Orsino for three days and their relationship is developing.

- Viola is favoured by Orsino, who has confided in her.
- Orsino enters and instructs Viola to visit Olivia and declare his love.
- Viola acknowledges that she has fallen for Orsino.

It appears that Orsino has taken Viola into his confidence, seeming to think that her apparent feminine qualities will influence Olivia. The **dialogue** is laden with **dramatic irony**: the audience is aware that Viola is indeed female, but Orsino remains oblivious. His final words to Viola are **ironic** given the prosperity that she will share when she does unite with Orsino.

Orsino's intimacy with Viola anticipates his later romantic feelings, but Viola's admission that she loves Orsino (delivered as an **aside**) is the significant event. Having to act as a messenger for the man she loves complicates the comedic problem of finding joy and shows the agony of love.

aside lines spoken directly by a character to the audience, which other onstage characters don't hear

dialogue the words spoken between characters

dramatic irony where the audience possesses more knowledge than the characters about events unfolding on stage

ironic where a secondary meaning is implied, often one that reveals the truth of a situation

Key quotations

> I have unclasp'd
> To thee the book even of my secret soul.
> *(Orsino)*

> Diana's lip
> Is not more smooth and rubious
> *(Orsino)*

> Yet, a barful strife!
> Whoe'er I woo, myself would be his wife.
> *(Viola)*

Act 1, Scene 5

In this lengthy scene, the audience meet two more characters: Feste, Olivia's **allowed fool**, who has just returned to the house, and Malvolio, her steward.

- Maria warns Feste that his unexplained absence will disappoint Olivia.
- Feste suggests to Olivia that her mourning is misplaced.
- Malvolio makes disparaging comments about Feste.

Feste's special position in the house permits him to use his **wit** to criticize Olivia, who appears to tolerate his playful yet barbed observations. Malvolio, who might be viewed as the play's **antagonist**, stands silently as this dialogue is played out, before criticizing Feste's views. Interestingly, Olivia defends Feste and suggests Malvolio is 'sick of self-love'. In the next segment of Act 1, Scene 5:

Olivia tolerates Feste as her allowed fool

- Olivia learns that a 'young gentleman' has arrived
- Viola enters and attempts to woo Olivia on behalf of Orsino
- Viola's romantic entreaties interest Olivia but she refuses Orsino's suit
- Olivia is attracted to Viola
- Olivia instructs Malvolio to encourage 'the youth' to return tomorrow, pretending that Viola has left a ring at the palace.

Olivia and Viola's dialogue, most of which occurs in private, offers two methods of wooing: the prepared speech which Olivia seems unimpressed by and Viola's more impassioned, personal declarations of passion. In the **soliloquy** near the end of the scene (starting 'What is your parentage?'), Olivia admits that falling in love is like catching the plague.

This scene creates the love triangle central to the comedy: Orsino loves Olivia who loves Viola, who in turn loves Orsino. Olivia seems transformed from the grieving countess we were led to expect from Valentine's description in Act 1, Scene 1. Olivia's ruse of the forgotten ring to make Viola return indicates the way that love's 'plague' can make even powerful people act in odd ways.

allowed fool a jester or fool who is permitted to make entertaining, yet often truthfully critical, comments

antagonist a character, often a villain, who acts as an obstacle in the narrative

complication an event that intensifies an existing conflict

soliloquy a speech delivered by a character alone on stage

wit verbal humour that relies on quick thinking and wordplay

Activity 3

Read Olivia and Viola's dialogue in the lines beginning **'The honourable lady of the house, which is she?'** up to **'Farewell, fair cruelty'** and consider:

- why Olivia initially thinks Viola is rude
- the ways in which Viola praises Olivia's features
- which part of Viola's speech seems most impassioned
- what has caused Olivia to fall for Viola.

Act 2, Scene 1

The action moves back to the coast and now we meet Sebastian, Viola's supposedly drowned brother and his companion Antonio.

- Sebastian is in despair, believing his sister is drowned.
- Antonio offers to be Sebastian's servant on his journey to Orsino's court.
- Sebastian departs on his own, but Antonio follows.

This brief scene allows the audience to see links between Sebastian and his sister in terms of their grief and physical similarity. It also introduces a further **complication** with the inclusion of the relationship between Antonio and Sebastian. Some directors present the relationship as one of homosexual desire on Antonio's part. His words 'I do adore thee so' appear passionate, and he is willing to risk his enemies' wrath at Orsino's court to follow Sebastian.

There are some interesting structural parallels between this scene and the preceding one: Olivia asks Fate to **'show thy force'** (*Act 1, Scene 5*) and this seems to occur immediately here, as Sebastian's appearance suggests that happier times are coming. Antonio's brief soliloquy at the end of the scene also parallels Olivia's declarations of love at the end of Act 1, Scene 5, alerting a perceptive reader that another love triangle – that of Olivia, Sebastian and Antonio – may emerge.

Key quotation

But come what may, I do adore thee so
That danger shall seem sport, and I will go.
(Antonio)

Act 2, Scene 2

This scene, set on a street, follows the story thread set up at the end of Act 1, Scene 5 where Olivia instructs Malvolio to return the ring supposedly left by Viola.

- Malvolio offers the ring to Viola but Viola doesn't recognize it.
- Malvolio throws it to the ground and exits.
- Viola realizes that Olivia is in love with her.

The impression that Malvolio is a joyless, churlish character is reinforced here. However, the most significant moment in this scene is Viola's recognition, delivered in her only soliloquy in the play, of the complexities of the situation between her, Olivia and Orsino. She offers views on the susceptibility of females to love.

Comedy usually suggests that things work out in the end through the benevolence of Fortune or the drive and desire of humans. Viola's **couplet** at the end of this scene suggests she will rely on luck and time to unravel matters.

> **couplet** two consecutive lines which rhyme

Key quotations

Poor lady, she were better love a dream.
(Viola)

          My master loves her dearly;
And I, poor monster, fond as much on him
(Viola)

O time, thou must untangle this, not I:
It is too hard a knot for me t'untie.
(Viola)

Activity 4

In her soliloquy beginning **'I left no ring with her'** (*Act 2, Scene 2*), Viola reflects on love and attraction. Consider:

- Why does Viola think Olivia has fallen for her? What, according to Viola, was the effect of this attraction upon Olivia?
- What impression of females and their logical and emotional qualities is given?

Act 2, Scene 3

The **subplot** of the play – the tricking of Malvolio – is established in Act 2, Scene 3. Shakespeare structures the scene first to show the audience the carefree behaviour of the knights with Feste, then to introduce Maria who sounds a note of caution about the revelry. Malvolio's entrance and reprimand provokes Maria to set about the business of puncturing Malvolio's pomposity.

- Sir Toby and Sir Andrew are enjoying a late-night drinking session.
- Feste enters and sings a melancholy song. They all sing.
- Maria warns them that Malvolio is displeased. They ignore her.
- Malvolio enters. They ignore his complaints.
- Malvolio exits and the plan is hatched by Maria.

The scene brings into focus the opposition between the riotous, carnival lifestyle of Sir Toby and the po-faced puritan values of Malvolio (for more on puritan values, see the panel on page 30). Sir Toby's raucous songs and disorderly behaviour contrast with Malvolio's uptight finger-wagging, seen in his threat to oversee the banishment of Sir Toby.

Malvolio's accusation that she is to blame for the **'uncivil rule'** gives Maria the reason to act. She seems to be another resourceful female, perceptively spotting Malvolio's weakness for self-love and determining a strategy to bring him down. Sir Toby's appreciation of Maria's qualities emerges in this scene.

> **subplot** a second strand to the story, which may be related to the ideas of the main plot

---

Key quotations

Have you no wit, manners, nor honesty
(Malvolio)

Dost thou think, because thou art virtuous, there shall be no more cakes and ale?
(Sir Toby)

She's a beagle, true-bred, and one that adores me
(Sir Toby)

 Activity 5

Is it possible to say who wields the most power out of the five characters in this scene? Consider:

- who has more status in the household: Malvolio or Sir Toby
- who is the more rebellious: Sir Toby or Maria
- how Feste fits into the power structure of the household.

Act 2, Scene 4

Viola's love for Orsino becomes more profound here. The **'barful strife'** she felt in Act 1, Scene 4 has magnified and is covertly expressed in her 'manly' chat with Orsino.

- Orsino enquires if Viola is in love and a discussion about women ensues.
- Feste sings a melancholy song about love and death.
- Viola tells of her 'sister', who was unable to express her love openly.
- Orsino once more sends Viola to woo Olivia.

The song of Feste (who appears to wander between the houses) brings together *Twelfth Night's* themes of love, suffering, death and music. Love's agony is also conveyed through dramatic irony in this scene: when Viola tells of her lover who is of the same age and complexion as the duke, it is clear she is referring to him. Although comic, it also creates **pathos** for Viola.

From **'My father had a daughter…'** to **'Sir, shall I to this lady?'**, we get a sense that Viola feels trapped. The very thing that allows her close to the duke – her disguise – prevents her from ever having him. Like the 'sister' Viola refers to (clearly herself), she fears she will pine away. Shakespeare's positioning of the audience is crucial here, because although we sympathize with Viola's plight, we know that Sebastian is alive and feel that things will work out, as they conventionally do in comedic texts.

> **pathos** the feeling of pity or sadness

Key quotations

Come away, come away death,
And in sad cypress let me be laid.
(Feste)

> *She never told her love,*
> *But let concealment, like a worm i' th' bud,*
> *Feed on her damask cheek*
> *(Viola)*

Activity 6

Explore Orsino and Viola's views on men and women in relation to love and emotions. You could use a table like the one below to record your notes.

	Orsino	Viola
Views about women	Females should be younger than their lovers: 'Let still the woman take / An elder than herself' (Act 2, Scene 4)	
Views about men		

Act 2, Scene 5

The action returns to the subplot initiated in Act 2, Scene 3 and we are shown the first stage in the duping of Malvolio. The setting is the garden of Olivia's house.

- Sir Toby, Sir Andrew and Fabian look forward to Malvolio's downfall.
- Maria enters and places a letter, supposedly from Olivia on the ground.
- Maria exits and the men conceal themselves.
- Malvolio enters and fantasizes aloud about his future power.
- He discovers the letter and falls for the trick.
- Malvolio exits and the plotters express their anticipation.

The scene allows for some physical comedy where Fabian, Sir Toby and Sir Andrew conceal themselves in a box tree and overhear Malvolio (who thinks he is alone) speculate about a future marriage to Olivia and the power he'll wield. His speech appears to confirm Maria's view of him as pompous, narcissistic and deserving of his forthcoming public embarrassment.

There is also verbal comedy in the bawdy humour of the letter, which references female genitalia. Malvolio's inability to grasp the joke (and the length of time it takes him to get the supposed references to himself) suggests that he is not only pompous but dim. The plot, to encourage him to wear yellow stockings and appear cross-gartered to (supposedly) impress Olivia, appears fitting punishment for the killjoy attitude he demonstrated in Act 2, Scene 3.

Sir Toby and his fellow pranksters spy on Malvolio

Maria's perceptiveness and cunning seem to impress Sir Toby, and once again, we note the developing attraction between this unlikely couple.

> **Key quotations**
>
> *Some are born great, some achieve greatness, and some have greatness thrust upon 'em.*
> (Malvolio)
>
> **I could marry this wench for this device.**
> (Sir Toby)

Activity 7

Look closely at Malvolio's fantasies from **'Having been three months married...'** up to **'What employment have we here?'** What do they reveal about his opinion of himself and his attitudes to others in the house?

Act 3, Scene 1

The opening of this scene is also set in Olivia's garden and features the further wooing of Olivia as requested by Orsino in Act 2, Scene 4.

- Viola meets Feste, who offers some pointed observations.
- She then meets Sir Toby and Sir Andrew.
- Olivia once more dismisses Orsino's pleas.
- Viola and Olivia both speak in coded terms about their situation.

Feste's apt remarks about husbands and fools early in the scene reveal his wit, and his comment about Viola being in want of a beard may well suggest that he (unlike everybody else) sees through her disguise. His cryptic remarks provide a structural link with the dialogue between Olivia and Viola later in this scene, which is also laden with concealed truths. Once again, the dramatic irony of the situation creates a sort of painful comedy, where the audience gets the coded references to Viola's womanhood. Olivia, however, explicitly expresses her feelings and, once more, the agony of love comes to the fore in the play.

Sir Andrew (who still foolishly sees himself a suitor to Olivia) appears to take some pointers from Viola's wooing techniques.

> **Key quotations**
>
> **This fellow is wise enough to play the fool**
> (*Viola*)
>
> **I have one heart, one bosom, and one truth,**
> **And that no woman has; nor never none**
> **Shall be mistress of it, save I alone.**
> (*Viola*)

Act 3, Scene 2

Sir Andrew, whose comic weakness and lack of self-awareness has been evident throughout the play, is in the process of being duped by Sir Toby.

- Sir Andrew threatens to leave, realizing he is wasting his time with Olivia.
- He is persuaded to fight Viola, who he sees as his rival for Olivia.
- Maria enters, stating that Malvolio has fallen into the trap.

Although he is a supposed friend, Sir Toby has some fun with Sir Andrew and assumes (wrongly as it turns out) that the duel will come to nothing. The joke appears to be that both Sir Andrew and Viola are cowards. There is a slightly darker edge hinted at here, however; it seems that Sir Toby has been enjoying the benefits of Sir Andrew's money, and this may explain why he is reluctant for Sir Andrew to leave. Maria's entrance serves as a trailer for the forthcoming attraction of Malvolio's humiliation. The subplot of *Twelfth Night* is rich in comic exploitation, power struggles and jokes at the expense of human folly or foolish conduct.

Activity 8

Look back at Sir Toby and Sir Andrew's interactions in Act 1, Scene 3; Act 2, Scenes 3 and 5; Act 3, Scenes 1 and 2. How would you describe their relationship? Is it exploitative? Explain your ideas using quotations from these scenes to support your arguments.

Act 3, Scene 3

This brief scene advances the audience's knowledge of Antonio's history and his loyalty to Sebastian. It is set in an unspecified street in Orsino's city.

● Sebastian is grateful that Antonio has followed him.

● Antonio's previous violence with Orsino's men puts him in danger.

● Antonio goes to his lodgings, leaving his purse with Sebastian.

The purse that Antonio gives Sebastian symbolizes the men's relationship in a way. Antonio's selfless attachment to Sebastian and his care for his friend's safety contrasts sharply with the other would-be lovers in the play, who appear driven by their own desires for pleasure or advancement.

Activity 9

Look closely at the nature of Antonio and Sebastian's relationship. Consider:

• Why does Antonio claim he followed Sebastian?

• What do you discover about Antonio's history?

• Why does Antonio give Sebastian his purse?

Act 3, Scene 4

Dramatic comedy usually has convoluted plots and in Act 3, Scene 4 many events occur to bring various plot strands together. This scene is set in the garden.

● Maria arrives and forewarns Olivia that Malvolio is possessed.

● Malvolio arrives smiling and dressed as the forged letter requested.

● Olivia requests Sir Toby to take care of an uncooperative Malvolio.

● Sir Toby decides to take him to a dark room.

dramatic comedy an amusing play that tells the story of how characters overcome problems and find happiness

In the first part of the scene, Olivia is deceived into thinking Malvolio is mad. On stage, this scene allows for much visual comedy, with Malvolio's outlandish costume and grotesquely demonstrative actions provoking laughter at his public humiliation. Sir Toby's decision to take him to a dark room – a traditional Elizabethan treatment for the insane – leads to a less light-hearted form of punishment. In the next segment of Act 3, Scene 4:

- Sir Andrew arrives with his letter challenging Viola to a duel.
- Sir Toby decides to trick both Sir Andrew and Viola.
- Olivia gives Viola a picture of herself to wear, telling her to visit again.
- Sir Toby and Fabian tell Viola that Sir Andrew is intent on harming her.
- Sir Andrew is clearly afraid of fighting.

Once again, the use of dramatic irony creates humour here. The audience is clearly aware of Sir Andrew's weakness, and laughter arises from the gap between Sir Toby's exaggerated description of Sir Andrew's skills and the reality. There is a cruelty here too, though, as Viola's fears seem real to her.

- Antonio enters thinking Viola is Sebastian.
- Sir Toby and Antonio draw swords. Two officers arrive to arrest Antonio.
- Antonio asks Viola for his purse. Viola is confused.
- Antonio is angry, and led away. Viola wonders if Sebastian is still alive.

Often misunderstanding in comedy is funny, but here it is painful for Antonio. It is in Act 3, Scene 4 that different aspects of the plot come together, and the possibility that a happy ending of sorts – Sebastian's return – is suggested.

Malvolio is tricked into wooing Olivia while wearing ridiculous clothing

---

Key quotations

Come, we'll have him in a dark room and bound. My niece is already in the belief that he's mad: we may carry it thus for our pleasure
(Sir Toby)

O if it prove,
Tempests are kind, and salt waves fresh in love!
(Viola)

Act 4, Scene 1

There are further misunderstandings in this scene that lead to mirth. The arrival of Sebastian and his physical similarity to Viola is at the root of this: every character in Act 4, Scene 1 mistakes Sebastian for his sister.

- Sebastian thinks Feste is a foolish fellow.
- Sir Andrew and Sebastian fight. Sir Toby and Sebastian draw swords.
- Olivia enters assuming her uncle is attacking Viola.
- Olivia dismisses Sir Toby, apologizing profusely to Sebastian.

Sir Toby's assumption that Sir Andrew will not be drawn into a fight is proven wrong here. In dialogue with Feste, Sebastian seems more aggressive than his sister, promising Feste **'worse payment'**. The comic drama of the scuffle (which is often played to emphasize Sir Andrew's ineptitude) and Sebastian's utter dismay at what people say to him leads to a lot of the humour.

Amid the hilarity, the key narrative event is Olivia's first meeting with Sebastian (whom she obviously assumes is Viola at this point), which leads to the resolution of some of the problems of the play. Sebastian appears to be delighted (if taken aback) with the attention given to him by Olivia.

Act 4, Scene 2

The plot against Malvolio reaches its dark conclusion in this scene.

- Maria instructs Feste to disguise himself as Sir Topas.
- From the dark room, Malvolio pleads with Sir Topas.
- Sir Toby wishes for an end to the trick on Malvolio.
- Feste promises to fetch a pen and paper for Malvolio.

In comedy, disguise and mistaken identity usually lead to humour and, while this scene can be played for laughs, some productions make a lot of the cruelty in the torment of Malvolio. His imprisonment and the assumption that he is mad is exacerbated by Feste's role-playing, where he switches between himself and the guise of Sir Topas. Sir Toby's wish for the prank to end is an interesting addition, but it seems that it is Sir Toby's wish to avoid further trouble with his niece, rather than sympathy for Malvolio, that provokes this.

 Activity 10

> Make a list of the characters who have been confused or deceived so far. Are misunderstandings always a cause for laughter?

Act 4, Scene 3

Comedy often relies on rapid plot development, sudden changes of fortune and the union of lovers to resolve the narrative. In Act 4, Scene 3:

- Sebastian reflects on his good luck.
- Olivia has arranged for a priest to hear the exchange of oaths.
- Sebastian happily agrees to this.

Sebastian's dismay at Olivia's love for him leads him to question whether she is mad. In his soliloquy, he reflects and decides to go along with his new-found fortune. This seems like a happy ending, but Olivia is unaware of her confusion between Sebastian and Viola, and he appears to agree to make a betrothal to a woman whose name he appears not to know. Although this exchange of oaths is binding, it isn't an actual marriage as such.

> **Key quotation**
>
> **Then lead the way, good father, and heavens so shine,**
> **That they may fairly note this act of mine!**
> (Olivia)

Activity 11

Look again at Sebastian's words from 'This is the air...' to 'But here the lady comes.' Why does Sebastian decide to accept Olivia's offer? How do you react to the suddenness and wisdom of his decision?

Act 5, Scene 1

In this final scene, disguises are thrown off and lovers are united. The different parts of the story are brought together and a resolution to the comedic problems occurs, yet there are some elements that are less joyous. In the first part of the scene, the characters still confuse Viola and Sebastian.

- Feste arrives carrying Malvolio's letter. He engages Orsino in dialogue.
- Antonio is brought on stage, having been arrested.
- Antonio defends himself and decries Viola (thinking she's Sebastian).
- Olivia enters, claiming Viola hasn't kept her promise.
- Orsino is outraged that Viola has pledged herself to Olivia.
- Viola pledges her love and loyalty to Orsino, astounding Olivia.
- A priest enters, confirming that Viola is betrothed to Olivia.

The quick interplay between the characters and their link to Viola add to the drama of the final scene. The love triangle reaches a **climax** here, with Viola suspected of playing false. Antonio's dismay at Viola's supposed denial of him also adds to the tension.

In the next segment of Act 5, Scene 1:

- An injured Sir Andrew enters, followed by Sir Toby, who is also hurt.
- Sebastian enters, to the amazement of Orsino and Olivia.
- Sebastian and Viola are reunited and the confusion is cleared up.
- Malvolio is sent for and his letter to Olivia is read aloud.
- Viola and Orsino are united, as are Olivia and Sebastian.
- A furious Malvolio enters and Fabian confesses the plot.
- We learn that Sir Toby and Maria have married.
- Feste taunts Malvolio, who storms off stage, threatening revenge.
- Feste closes the play with a melancholy song.

The comic violence experienced by the knights relieves the tension and paves the way for the arrival of Sebastian, leading to a series of **revelations** for the characters. The comedic rapid pairing of lovers resolves the plot, with the less likely union of Sir Toby and Maria mentioned as an after-thought. Antonio and Sir Andrew aren't as fortunate in love, and Malvolio's bitterness and possible revenge remain. The song of Feste ends the play on a less happy note.

climax the high point of a narrative
revelation an event in a story where a truth or a secret is discovered

Key quotations

I'll sacrifice the lamb that I do love,
To spite a raven's heart within a dove.
(Orsino)

Here is my hand; you shall from time be
Your master's mistress.
(Orsino)

I'll be reveng'd on the whole pack of you!
(Malvolio)

Writing about plot

Once you have read *Twelfth Night*, read it again in conjunction with the notes in this section. Any parts of the play with which you are less confident need to be mastered.

Knowing the text really well allows you the freedom to select the very best quotations and references to explain the point you are making. Students who are unsure of parts of the text often rely on the scenes they know best, even if they aren't relevant to the question they are being asked. This means their answer will not be as good as it could be.

Structure

Writing about the structure of a text is different from focusing simply on the events of the play. When you explore the plot, you are considering the events which happen. When you think about structure, you are thinking about the order and manner in which those events are revealed to the audience.

You will have noticed some basic structural aspects already, such as the division of the play into acts and scenes, and the way in which the action switches between the houses of Orsino and Olivia. As well as thinking about the way the story is arranged at the level of the whole plot, it is also useful to analyse the way action is structured *within* scenes.

Conflict

Dramatic plots are driven by conflict. *Twelfth Night* explores characters' internal and external conflicts. Some of the problems the characters face are brought upon them by external forces, events or the actions of others, whereas some problems appear to be self-generated. In comedic texts, an initial event or events signals the start of disorder and conflict. The acts that follow intensify the conflict(s), complicating the problem before a comedic resolution in which issues are usually smoothed over and a sense of order emerges.

The structure of drama usually moves through complication to climax to resolution. In dramatic comedy, there is usually a restoration of order. The closing scene often shows the community coming together and healing any wounds in the interest of harmony and stability. There is a sense of optimism, suggesting that things work out in the end and that any villainous behaviour is corrected or punished. Some form of communal celebration – usually a marriage or dance – occurs, creating a sense of unity and uplift.

You will have noticed that *Twelfth Night* opens at a point *after* several key events have happened. The **backstory** of the shipwreck that separates Viola and Sebastian has occurred, Olivia's father and brother have died, and Orsino's unsuccessful wooing of Olivia has begun. The play's dramatic focus is the way in which the protagonists overcome the problems of loss and unrequited love.

---

backstory events that have happened before the play begins

Activity 12

Using the plot summaries in the first part of this chapter, explore the disruptions that occur in the structure of the story. Identify:

- the initial problem(s) in the early scenes
- the types of conflicts experienced by all characters
- where the complications occur and how they develop the problems
- what climactic moments occur and where
- which events bring about the resolution.

You could use a diagram such as a flow chart or spidergram to help you map out the events and make links between them.

Plot and subplot

Unlike dramatic tragedy, which tends to focus the action on one central character, comedy can often have a wider array of characters and more complicated plots. Viola may be the protagonist of *Twelfth Night*, but arguably Orsino and Olivia may also deserve the term too, given their importance to the ending. Comedies can appear 'busy' and this can be seen in the dizzying array of events in Act 5, Scene 1, which features a series of entrances, exits, dialogue between sets of characters and a rapid resolution.

The two main story strands of *Twelfth Night*, which are termed 'plot' and 'subplot' in the summaries above, can also be considered in terms of their importance to the structure of the play. Some parts of the story have a romantic or serious aspect, exploring love relationships, and some parts are comic, adding humour to the play. As you begin to explore the balance between the serious and light-hearted elements, you should consider if it is possible to easily categorize the play into romantic scenes and comic scenes.

Activity 13

a) Look again at the events in each scene and note the parts that deal with romantic ideas and parts that are comic. You could use a table like this:

Where	Romantic/serious elements	Comic elements
Act 1, Scene 1	<ul><li>Orsino's melancholy</li><li>Orsino's love for Olivia</li><li>Olivia's grief and mourning</li></ul>	<ul><li>the pun on 'hart', which eases the mood of the scene</li></ul>

b) Now review your notes and explore:

- What is the balance between serious and comic moments in the play?
- Is it too simplistic to say that the main plot deals with romantic/serious matters and the subplot is simply comic?
- At which point(s) do plot and subplot come together?

The structural function of characters

In the chapter on characterization and roles you will explore the attributes of characters, but it is useful here to consider the role of characters in relation to the story. Shakespeare uses his characters for structural purposes: for instance, characters are often brought into stories to initiate problems or to act as a contrast. They often make **metaphorical** journeys in stories and, particularly in comedy, they often learn valuable lessons or make transformations.

An example: Sebastian

The main function of Sebastian is to act as an **agent of resolution**. His appearance allows the problematic love triangle between Orsino, Olivia and Viola to be resolved in Act 5, Scene 1. He also brings happiness to his sister, who presumes that he is dead. It is worth noting that we hear about Sebastian before we see him: Viola's account of him in Act 1, Scene 2 leads the audience to anticipate his appearance later in the play, but it isn't until Act 2, Scene 1 that his survival is confirmed. From that point on, the interest lies largely in how he comes to arrive at Orsino's court and the confusions that emerge. The side story of Antonio's affection for him also adds a contrast to the main plot.

Sebastian, like many of the characters in the play can be seen in relation to another, in this case, his sister. Links are made between not only their appearance, but also their sorrow and resourceful qualities. Sebastian also aids the comedy too: his physical similarity to Viola adds to the confusion and he delivers a comic comeuppance to Sir Toby and Sir Andrew in the final scene. Unlike other characters, it's debatable whether Sebastian develops as a character during the story: he certainly finds happiness and also his sister, but the focus is more on his literal journey than his emotional one.

> **agent of resolution** a force, event or character that helps to bring about an end to the problem(s) in the story
>
> **metaphor** a comparison between entities implying that one thing is another

Activity 14

Using the example of Sebastian above as a template, write about the structural function of Viola, Orsino, Olivia, Sir Toby, Malvolio and Feste. For each character, consider:

- when they first appear in the play and their position at the end of it
- whether they develop as a character and what, if anything, they learn
- whether they can be contrasted or compared with another character
- what they contribute to the ideas in the play.

The positioning of the audience

Another way to analyse structure is to consider who knows what, and when. This can be done in relation to characters and audience. For instance, Viola and Sebastian only discover that the other is alive in the final scene, yet the audience suspects from Act 1, Scene 1 (given that this is a comedy) that Sebastian is still alive, a fact confirmed in the next act. The placement of the audience in a position of superiority in terms of knowledge means that we are less concerned about *whether* problems work out, and focus instead on *how* they are resolved.

Sebastian acts as an agent of resolution, and confusion, especially when both his and Viola's parts are played by male actors.

Activity 15

In the chapter on language you will look closely at dramatic irony and its effect, but for now explore the audience's possession of knowledge in the play. Consider:

- if there is ever a point in the play when the audience fears for a character or wonders what might happen to them

- whether the audience's superior knowledge causes them to feel sympathy or simply amusement.

imagery the use of visual or other vivid language to convey ideas

symbolism the use of an object that represents someone or something else

Writing about structure

Exploring the larger structural features of a play, such as where and how the action starts, how the resolution of the story is brought about, and crucially, when the characters – and audience – discover key information will help you to see the way in which Shakespeare has shaped the narrative.

Smaller structural aspects such as dramatic irony, **symbolism**, **imagery**, contrast and dialogue will also allow you to demonstrate your understanding of the play at a more analytical level. The ability to analyse the structural features of a text will give your answers much more depth and quality.

Studying the context of a piece of literature means thinking about the surrounding beliefs and cultural ideas that existed when the work was written. You must also consider how your own personal contexts in the world you live in affect how you might read and interpret a play. In many ways, when deciding on how you view *Twelfth Night*, the contexts of reception (the point where you personally 'receive' or experience the play) are as important as the contexts in which it was written.

The literary sources of the play

Today, literary works are expected to be original; in Shakespeare's time, this convention wasn't part of the literary culture. Instead, writers usually adapted existing stories, combining ideas from several sources to produce new texts. One of the sources of *Twelfth Night* may well be *Gl'Ingannati* (1537), an anonymous Italian play whose title means 'The Deceived'. Another text that appears to have some similarities is Barnaby Riche's tale *Apolonius and Silla*, contained in Riche's *His Farewell to Military Profession* (1581).

Gl'Ingannati

Several versions of this text exist. There are numerous plot similarities with *Twelfth Night*. In the original play, Flamminio loves Isabella, but Isabella loves Lelia who has disguised herself as a boy called Fabio. Lelia is in love with Flamminio, her master. Lelia's brother Fabrizio is mistaken for Lelia. In the end, he marries Isabella and Lelia marries Flamminio.

Apolonius and Silla

This tale forms part of a collection of romantic stories. In the play, the beautiful Silla falls in love with Apolonius and follows him to Constantinople, but a storm causes the ship to break up. She adopts male clothing and changes her name to Silvio, which is also the name of her brother. Silla serves at the court of Apolonius, who is wooing the wealthy widow Julina. Silvio acts as messenger and Julina falls in love with Silla. The problems are resolved by two marriages.

Shakespeare's own comedies

Shakespeare's own earlier work might also be considered as contributing to the design of *Twelfth Night*. By the time Shakespeare wrote the play, he had produced several earlier comedies and some of the plotlines of these plays have echoes in *Twelfth Night*. For instance, *The Comedy of Errors* (1594) contains a shipwreck in which two identical (male) twins are separated then reunited at the end. Other plays have similar narrative threads.

In *An Introduction to Shakespeare's Comedies* (1973), Patrick Swinden notes the following ideas about *Twelfth Night*:

> Shakespeare seems to have entered into the spirit of the occasion by putting all his best ideas to work. *Twelfth Night* is a collection of self-borrowings, standing at one end of Shakespeare's achievement in the genre of romantic comedy [...] In this respect, as in others, *Twelfth Night* is the crown of Shakespeare's achievement in romantic comedy.

> No other comedy has so clear a contrast between the romantic affairs of the principals and the feasting, drinking and merry-making of the sub-plot [...] In fact it is inaccurate to call the action involving Tony, Sir Andrew, Feste, Maria and Malvolio a sub-plot. Shakespeare invented it himself and added it to the story he had taken from a much earlier sixteenth-century Italian play.

Activity 1

a) Read plot summaries of *The Two Gentleman of Verona, Love's Labour's Lost, The Merry Wives of Windsor* and *As You Like It*. What links can you find between the plots of these plays and those in *Twelfth Night*?

b) Given the amount of 'self-borrowings', is there anything fresh about *Twelfth Night*? Does the ending offer anything different from previous works?

c) How far do you agree with Swinden's view that the plot strand involving the plot against Malvolio constitutes more than a mere subplot? When you watch the play, is it the romantic storyline or the mischief-making that holds your attention?

Festivity and carnival

Twelfth night, the day the play takes its name from, falls on 6 January, which is the end of the twelve days of Christmas known as Christmastide. It also marks the day when the magi – the three wise men – visited the baby Jesus. Twelfth night is generally regarded as the last opportunity to celebrate during the holiday period before returning to the world of work and normality. The play's title probably refers to the day on which the play was first performed and, although the time setting of the play is indeterminate, referencing both **'midsummer madness'** *(Act 3, Scene 4)* and **'the twelfth day of December'** *(Act 2, Scene 3)*, the play has a sense of festive playfulness in which the normal patterns of everyday life are suspended. The spirit of carnival may be seen in the text.

Carnival

This term was used by Russian critic Bakhtin to describe the freedom that comes from the temporary suspension of hierarchy. It is the name of an annual festival involving music, dancing, processions and masquerade, usually celebrated during the week before Lent in Roman Catholic countries.

The festive period of the past was (as today) given over to consumption of food and drink. Frivolity was the norm, rather than the sober behaviour of the working week. The period was sometimes termed the 'Feast of Fools' and in some institutions, a Lord of Misrule was appointed, who organized lively, hedonistic behaviour. Pranks, trickery and deceptions were commonplace and a kind of merry madness was enjoyed by everyday working people.

Lord of Misrule

The Lord of Misrule was a role specifically appointed to someone to manage the Christmas festivities in various prestigious locations, such as the houses of great noblemen, the law schools of the Inns of Court and in many colleges at Oxford University and Cambridge University. The Lord of Misrule would arrange and direct all Christmas entertainment, including parades, plays and feasts. The Lord of Misrule could also be called the Abbot or King Of Misrule.

The Lord of Misrule was in charge of all festivities – and mischief

How is the festive spirit reflected in the play? Make a list of the tricks, pranks and hedonistic behaviour in the play.

- Which characters are responsible for these actions?
- Do you think the play always celebrates these actions?

Power and misrule

In some ways, the festive period was a rejection of the strictures of work and authority, with the Lord of Misrule holding power over the household and flouting rules that were in place during the rest of the year. An exchange of power occurred, and hierarchies – power structures – were inverted for a time.

Twelfth night itself had other customs such as the placing of a bean inside a cake; the finder of the bean was then elected 'Bean King' and assumed charge of the festivities for the evening. Bean kings could well be servants and so the custom often handed power to those who were powerless during the year. For a brief time, a servant may have had authority over his master and a topsy-turvy reign existed where madness flourished. There is still a sense of this custom today when bosses make cakes for their employees as a holiday approaches or army officers cook Christmas dinner for their soldiers.

The rebellious quality of the period could give rise to actions that might be considered discourteous. In *Shakespeare's Festive Comedy* (1959), C.L. Barber noted that 'In the customs which center on a Lord of Misrule, the rougher pleasures of defiance and **mockery** are uppermost'. Twelfth night also marked the end of the festive period so was tinged with a sense of melancholy that the fun was ending. The conclusion of the evening signalled a return to the usual order so, in some ways, the carnival spirit was short-lived and served to remind working people that joy is brief and festivity is a temporary illusion.

mockery making fun of something or someone, drawing attention to aspects of their behaviour that seem odd or amusing

Activity 3

a) Which characters in the play embody the spirit of misrule?

b) Which actions in the play might be deemed rebellious, defiant or cruel?

c) Where in the play do servants enjoy power over their superiors?

d) Do superior characters willingly accept attempts to subvert their power?

e) Is there any sense that the playful actions are tinged with sadness?

Puritanism

Standing in opposition to the pleasure-seeking world of carnival was Puritanism. Historically, Puritanism was a movement within the Church of England that aimed to change church practices. It developed a reputation for austerity. In the play, Malvolio is viewed by some of the characters and audience as the embodiment of a joyless Puritan who disapproves of fun.

Malvolio's puritanical behaviour ensures his unpopularity and makes him the target of Maria's joke

Puritanism

In the late 16th and 17th centuries, this religious reform movement of English Protestants sought to remove any remaining elements of Roman catholic church practice (such as ceremonies, church ornaments, the use of musical instruments, and in some cases 'popery') which they considered corrupt. In doing this, they believed to 'purify' the Church of England. In the 17th century, Puritans were recognised to have a moral and religious earnestness that informed their whole way of life. Through the church reformation, they intended to make their lifestyle the pattern of the whole nation. This consequently contributed to civil war in England and to the establishment of colonies in America as working models of the Puritan way of life.

The word 'puritan' has come to describe somebody who lives by strict moral codes and is opposed to luxury.

The adjective 'puritanical' is used to describe a strict, moral and often miserable attitude to life. Puritans are **caricatured** as humourless, smugly religious characters, who approach life in a black-and-white manner and take a dim view of those who enjoy the livelier side of life. The Puritans of the past opposed the non-religious excess of Christmas and also sought to close down theatres, deeming them places of sin, which came to pass in 1642.

caricatured made fun of through exaggerating the appearance or manner of someone or something

Activity 4

Malvolio clashes with Feste in Act 1, Scene 5 and with Sir Toby in Act 2, Scene 3. Look carefully at those scenes, exploring the exchanges and noting Malvolio's attitudes. You could use a table like the one below to record your observations:

Location	Quotation	Analysis
Act 1, Scene 5 (Feste)	I saw him put down the other day with an ordinary fool, that has no more brain than a stone.	Malvolio takes exception to Feste's criticism of Olivia's mourning and suggests Feste has no wit.

Activity 5

Look again at Maria's description of Malvolio in Act 2, Scene 3 from **'The devil a Puritan…'** to **'find notable cause to work'**. Is her description of Malvolio in these lines proved correct by his actions later in the play?

The clash between carnival and Lent

One way of reading the play is to see it as exploring the opposing forces of revelry and restraint, as represented in the characters of Sir Toby and Malvolio. The attitude of carnival is the polar opposite of Lent, a six-week period in the Christian calendar when people give up luxuries and repent past sins. Lent (which ends on the Sunday before Easter) is often accompanied by fasting.

Sir Toby often indulges in excessive behaviour. He is a drinker, he flirts with Maria, encourages dancing and violence, sets up pranks and appears to care little for his niece's grief. Malvolio is often seen as the butt of the humour in the play. The term 'butt' derives from archery and has come to mean 'a target for ridicule'. In *Shakespeare's Festive Comedy* (1959), C.L. Barber noted that:

Sir Toby's character is the antithesis of Malvolio's

 The butts in the festive plays exhibit their unnaturalness by being kill-joys […] Behind the laughter at the butts there is always a sense of solidarity about pleasure, a communion embracing the merrymakers in the play and the audience, who have gone on holiday in going to a comedy.

Activity 6

a) Do you agree with the view that the characters and the audience unite in laughter against Malvolio?

b) Consider whether Shakespeare always invites us to side with Sir Toby.

Key quotations

My masters, are you mad? Or what are you?
(Malvolio, Act 2, Scene 3)

I'll go burn some sack, 'tis too late to go to bed now.
(Sir Toby, Act 2, Scene 3)

The Petrarchan lover

The feelings of Orsino and the way in which he views Olivia are an example of courtly love, as represented in the sonnets of Petrarch (1304–74). The concept of courtly love focused on the female as a highly sought-after, beautiful, refined lady who powerful, chivalrous males would adore and compete for. Petrarch was a poet whose work has become synonymous with the heightened feelings of the male lover.

The Petrarchan male lover was a blend of the strong, masculine type and the sensitive, poetic male who would place his idealized lover on a pedestal. The lady was portrayed as cruel, rejecting her suitor and consigning him to a life of melancholic misery. The love object of Petrarch's poetry, Laura, was portrayed as a beautiful, unattainable female whose qualities caused a type of lovelorn misery in the would-be male lover.

Read the following conventions of Petrarchan love poetry as identified by Michael Delahoyde. The poet-lover:

- addresses a lady (corresponding to Petrarch's Laura), who often has a classical name like Stella or Delia
- praises his mistress's unrivalled qualities using descriptions of beauty supplied by Petrarch: 'golden hair', 'ivory breast', 'ruby lips'. She is the object and image of love.
- presents himself as ardent and impetuous
- dwells only on the subjective experience of the misery of being in love, for example, praying for sleep to allay the pain
- employs contradictory and **oxymoronic** phrases and images: for example, freezing and burning, binding and freedom
- disclaims credit for poetic merits: he claims that the inspiration of his mistress is what makes the poetry good
- promises to protect the youth of his lady and his own love against time (as though the poetry itself is immortalizing)
- is continuously at work on his personal drama.

> **oxymoron** a figure of speech that combines contradictory words or images

Activity 7

Look closely at Orsino's feelings as expressed in Act 1, Scene 1 in light of the Petrarchan love conventions identified here. Consider:

- how he portrays Olivia
- how he represents his own feelings
- how he regards his own qualities.

> **Key quotations**
>
> So full of shapes is fancy,
> That it alone is high fantastical.
> *(Orsino, Act 1, Scene 1)*
>
> Away before me to sweet beds of flowers!
> Love-thoughts lie rich when canopied with bowers.
> *(Orsino, Act 1, Scene 1)*

The play never shows us the backstory of the meeting between Olivia and Orsino that he refers to in Act 1, Scene 1, but whether he does actually know Olivia very well at all is debatable. His image of her fits the conventional model of the Petrarchan love object and his main contact with her is through messengers.

Activity 8

Is Orsino's view of Olivia confirmed elsewhere in the play? Look again at how Olivia is represented:

- by the Captain in Act 1, Scene 2
- by Feste in Act 1, Scene 5.

Activity 9

Is there a difference between the public reputation of Olivia and the Olivia we see interacting with the rest of her household in Act 1, Scene 5? Consider:

- the conversation between Olivia and the rest of her household
- how Olivia responds to Viola's arrival
- the nature of the dialogue between Olivia and Viola.

Orsino's journey from would-be Petrarchan lover to a character who finds (arguably) real feelings is one of the hallmarks of the play. The Orsino the audience meet in Act 1, Scene 1 seems static and stereotypical. In *Shakespeare: Twelfth Night* (1980), J.M. Gregson remarks that the Orsino we meet in Act 1, Scene 1 is self-indulgent and used partly by Shakespeare to mock courtly love conventions.

Tips for assessment

When writing about characters, look at how they are constructed. Don't fall into the trap of treating characters as 'real' people. Instead, explore what the playwright has them saying and doing: remember that characters serve a function.

Activity 10

In light of J.M. Gregson's view about Orsino, explore the idea that Shakespeare invites you to see the limitations and absurdity of the Petrarchan lover. Consider whether:

- Orsino seems more focused on his own drama than on Olivia
- he appears to enjoy wallowing in feelings of melancholy
- you (as a 21st-century reader) find his posturing laughable.

Gender and sexuality

Comedic texts focus on matters of love and gender, often inviting the audience to consider ideas about masculinity and femininity. The biological categories 'male' and 'female' denote the bodily differences between men and women, but concepts of 'masculinity' and 'femininity' are socially constructed. This means that society decides what 'being a man' and 'being a woman' constitute. Stereotypically, men are viewed as strong, logical and courageous, and women as maternal, emotional and gentle. Although generalized, these are recognizable representations of gender in some literary texts.

Shakespeare's representation of gender and his playfulness with cross-dressing is a feature of his comedic work. *As You Like It*, for instance, features Rosalind, who assumes the role of Ganymede, disguising herself as a boy and manipulating Orlando, the man she ends up marrying. The freedom that this fluid gender identity allows lends some power to the female, placing her in the role of active wooer, rather than passive recipient of male attention.

Does Olivia fall in love with a man or a woman?

Twelfth Night clearly plays with disguise and gender identity. In doing so, comic moments arise, which provide an opportunity to consider how rigidly defined the categories of gender are, and whether in fact love and attraction are bound by heterosexuality or whether identity is fixed at all.

Activity 11

Make a list of characters in the play and the extent to which they conform to socially conventional versions of masculinity and femininity. Consider their actions, words and (where applicable) their experiences of love and attraction.

You could use a table like the one below to record your notes.

Character	Analysis in relation to gender
Olivia	• Perceived by Orsino to embody female perfection: viewed as desirable and chaste. Initially unwilling to engage with suitors – a sense of sexual disinterest • Has power over her household and the men within it – but this is a result of the deaths of her father and brother • Falls in love with a woman dressed as a man and seems attracted to Viola's feminine prettiness • Succumbs to 'love's plague' – becomes emotional and also determined to secure Viola's attention • Takes an active role – woos Viola in Act 3, Scene 1

Comedic playfulness and gender

Comedies allow space for experimentation. They often feature characters whose journey includes some sort of transformation. *Twelfth Night* commences with a traditional heterosexual scenario – Orsino's attraction to Olivia – and very quickly introduces the playful idea of a cross-dressed heroine who causes the audience to reflect on the nature of desire. In the world of the play, of course, Olivia is convinced that she is attracted to a male and yet at the end of Act 1, Scene 5 the audience note that her attraction is based on the physical and personal qualities of Viola rather than any traditionally masculine aspects.

Although he believes he has employed a male, Orsino too notes the feminine qualities of Viola and purposely sends her to woo Olivia, believing that her **'constellation is right apt / For this affair'** *(Act 1, Scene 4)*. An intimacy has developed between Orsino and Viola, and some productions use action and body language to suggest that Orsino's feelings towards Viola in the early scenes of the play are more than platonic. In doing so, Orsino's journey takes on an interesting shape, as he moves from the fiercely heterosexual character of Act 1, Scene 1 to a character confused by the nature of his feelings towards a young man. The play's resolution returns us to a state of 'normality' where heterosexual pairings occur, but it could well be argued that the very things that attract Orsino and Olivia to Viola and Sebastian are not exclusive to their gender.

Masculinity and homosexuality

It's important not to generalize about society's attitudes when dealing with contextual material – although you might assume that the era you live in has an enlightened attitude towards matters such as sexual orientation and race, you will be aware that not everybody adopts similar attitudes. Broadly speaking, however, in 16th-century England attitudes towards homosexuality were intolerant.

In *Homosexuality and the Signs of Male Friendship in Elizabethan England* (1990), Alan Bray states 'homosexuality was […] regarded with a readily expressed horror'. He goes on to say that homosexuality was seen as a crime, not only of a sexual nature, but also a political and religious one. There was also a clear distinction made between homosexuality and the more acceptable masculine friendship, even though a physical closeness between male friends was commonplace. Writing about the word 'bedfellow', Bray notes 'this was a society where most people slept with someone else and where the rooms of a house led casually one into the other and servants mingled with their masters'.

Although the cross-dressed attractions between Olivia, Viola and Orsino might be seen as knowingly comic, some productions and readings of the play explore Sebastian and Antonio's relationship as homosexual attraction on the part of the latter. Whether this is justified by the text and whether it adds a welcome complexity to the story is worth considering further.

Activity 12

If you were asked to direct a production of the play, how would you instruct the actors to play the relationship between Antonio and Sebastian? Look closely at Act 2, Scene 1; Act 3, Scene 3; and Act 5, Scene 1. Should they be merely intimate masculine friends or is there any merit in suggesting a repressed or even overt homosexual aspect to their relationship?

Activity 13

In Act 3, Scene 2, Sir Toby and Fabian jokingly suggest to Sir Andrew that he needs to be a real man to impress Olivia and have **'fire in your heart'** *(Act 3, Scene 2)*. Are there any male characters in this play who exhibit traditionally masculine qualities and, if so, are they held up as models of valour or are they ridiculed?

Writing about context

Be careful not to deal with context in a generalized way. Although it's possible to talk about the general beliefs held by Elizabethans, avoid making sweeping statements that assume all Elizabethans were racist, for example. As a comparison, you might think about all of the people you know and consider whether their views can be lumped together as 'what 21st-century people think' or whether people have a variety of viewpoints, regardless of the times in which they live.

It's always best to couch any points you make about context in tentative terms and let the contextual material arise naturally from the play, rather than 'force' contexts on the play. Simply expressing some facts about contexts of production will not add much to your writing. Any writing about context should be linked to the events of the play. The material in this section of the book has shown how to link contextual ideas to the play. Using these methods in your own writing will help you to handle context effectively.

Twelfth Night as a comedy

One very important context against which *Twelfth Night* can be read is that of literary genre. Genre refers to the text type or category a piece of writing can be placed in. By putting a label on a text, readers can begin to interpret it: they come to expect certain events to occur. In everyday life, 'comedy' equates to comic (i.e. funny) events in life or on television. But in literary terms, comedy is a stylized representation of amusing events with a set of comedic conventions, which a playwright can work within or against (or both).

In *Poetics*, Aristotle (384–322 BCE) described comedy as the imitation of inferior actions and considered comedy as beneficial to society. Comedy as a form has developed over the centuries, sometimes focusing on crude humour and sometimes offering amusing, intelligent criticism of people in power.

Sir Toby and Sir Andrew are obviously comic characters

Activity 1

Research the literary history of comedy. Read summaries of early comedies by playwrights such as Aristophanes, and later dramatists such as Goldsmith and Wilde. You might also consider TV comedy such as *Fawlty Towers*, *The Office* and *The Inbetweeners*.

- What links do you find between the plot of *Twelfth Night* and the events of other comedies you have explored?

- What are the differences between the status of the characters in Shakespeare's play and those in more modern TV comedy?

The conventions of comedy

Although there are many different types of comedy and the genre varies over time, there is a loose set of conventions for literary comedy. These can include the following:

1. a plot that is driven by the protagonists' desire to find love, happiness or security

2. a resourceful character, a comic hero/heroine who succeeds as a result of their ingenuity

3. a series of amusing moments that rely on silly actions, absurd situations and sexual jokes

4. an element of good luck, which suggests that fortune is on the side of the protagonist(s)

5. the suggestion of disaster or potential tragedy, which is averted or rectified

6. the use of disguise, trickery and misunderstandings

7. a sense that the characters have learned something on their journeys in the story – some form of transformation

8. an ending that suggests the characters have found happiness, usually in the form of love.

Activity 2

Using the eight-point list above, explore how far *Twelfth Night* adheres to these conventions. Identify where in the play these comedic elements occur.

Comedic element	How *Twelfth Night* follows or does not follow the convention
1	The initial plot strand focuses on Orsino's unrequited love and shows how he discovers that Olivia, who he thought he wanted, isn't the solution to his unhappiness. Olivia, Viola and Sebastian aren't necessarily looking for love (although they find it) and are instead learning to cope with grief or a new environment.

The resourceful protagonist

Comedy tends to suggest that humans have the power to make their own happiness so the inclusion of protagonists who have resourceful attributes – creativity, optimism and agency – reinforces this message. The image of the character who through personal skills can overcome obstacles and potential disaster is a seductive one, and presents the audience with a version of humanity at its best. Comedy suggests that people survive and thrive.

Viola does seem resourceful. Consider her journey in the play. She:

- accepts her displacement and sets about trying to make things better by adopting a disguise and seeking employment
- rapidly finds herself taken into the powerful Orsino's confidence
- gains access to Olivia, distracts her from grief and causes her to fall in love
- takes an optimistic attitude towards her brother's supposed death
- wins the heart of the man she is attracted to.

Activity 3

a) It could be argued that it is fortune, rather than Viola's resourcefulness, which brings about her happy ending. To what extent do you agree with this view?

b) Is there any sense in which Olivia and Orsino are resourceful? Explain your ideas.

---

farce comedy based on the pursuit of love, sex or money; it includes fast-paced absurd events

slapstick comedy that relies on comic violence and accidents

Types of fool

Comedy requires idiots, clowns and fools. The human impulse to laugh at the silly behaviour of others appears instinctive. Whether the actions of others are unintentionally or intentionally silly, humour is generated from the accidents, misapprehensions and wit of such characters. Sometimes characters are made fools of and sometimes they choose to act the fool.

Different types of fooling are seen in *Twelfth Night:* the manner in which Feste, the allowed fool, uses humour to entertain differs from the sort of clowning performed by Sir Toby and Sir Andrew. In *The Cambridge Introduction to Comedy* (2009), Eric Weitz notes some key types of foolery (see page 41).

Clowning: [Clowns] allow a universal identification with uphill struggle. At the same time they encourage, through laughter, an assertion of superiority. Despite unswerving determination and fantastic invention, clowns spend most of their time failing.

Comic pairing: The comic team or double act bases its humour strategies on the dialogue […] A crucial element offered by the two-performer configuration lies in relationship. Oppositions between personality and status supply vital hues to the joking transaction.

Fools and madmen: A dim character may display cracked logic or judgement […] The 'wise fool' on the Elizabethan stage exercises a licence – obligation, in fact – to dispense cheeky advice, especially by confounding the laws of reason.

The trickster figure: [The] trickster is a personification of mischief, wholly adult in body and appetite, yet possessed of a childlike indulgence in whim and desire.

 Activity 4

Look again at the behaviour of Sir Toby Belch in the play. Using Weitz's descriptions and the information on the Lord of Misrule in the chapter on context, consider the type of fool Sir Toby represents. Look closely at:

- his exchange with Maria in Act 1, Scene 3
- his brief appearance in Act 1, Scene 5
- his interaction with Malvolio in Act 2, Scene 3
- his manipulation of Sir Andrew as it is shown in Act 3, Scene 2.

 Activity 5

Explore the idea that Sir Andrew is a clown who spends most of his time failing. Look again at:

- his dialogue with Maria in Act 1, Scene 3
- his sense of self in Act 1, Scene 3
- his bravado in Act 2, Scene 5 and Act 3, Scene 4
- his interactions with Sebastian in Act 4, Scene 1 and Act 5, Scene 1.

Physical comedy and farce

The comic pairing of Sir Toby and Sir Andrew leads to some moments of physical comedy and **farce**. Their appearance is entertaining visually: in most performances, Sir Toby is a round, red-faced drunk, which contrasts comically with the lean, old and white-faced Sir Andrew. The dancing, drinking and singing and the inclusion of farcical events such as the confusion over the fight add a touch of **slapstick**.

Activity 6

Look closely at how the humour operates in Act 3, Scene 4, where Malvolio reads the letter while Sir Toby, Sir Andrew and Fabian are hidden in the box tree. Is the laughter based on simple physical comedy, or are there subtler aspects to the humour?

Wit and satire

Feste is clearly a different type of fool, one whose wit, logic and playfulness with language marks him out as perceptive. His role as an allowed fool gives him free rein to offer pointed criticism, which causes thought as well as laughter. In Act 1, Scene 3 he constructs an argument to suggest that Olivia is a fool for mourning her brother when she should be happy that he is in heaven. During the course of the play Feste not only criticizes Olivia, but draws attention to Orsino's capriciousness, and ridicules Viola's appearance, perhaps even seeing through her disguise. Some of his comments in the early scenes suggest he can see the relationship between Maria and Sir Toby. Feste functions as a truth-teller, offering wisdom and censure to others.

Part of Feste's skill is the manner in which he plays with word meaning and puns, as this exchange from Act 3, Scene 1 shows:

VIOLA: Save thee, friend, and thy music! Dost thou live by thy tabor?
FESTE: No, sir, I live by the church.
VIOLA: Art thou a churchman?
FESTE: No such matter, sir. I do live by the church, for I do live at my house, and my house doth stand by the church.
(Act 3, Scene 1)

Feste draws attention, through corrupting the meaning of words, to the instability of language and its inexactness. His riddles and deliberate distortion of meaning seem to echo a wider theme of the play: that life (and language too) are unstable concepts. In a play where gender identity is at times unfixed, Feste's aim seems to be to undermine, subvert and suggest that the world is a random place where things that appear to be stable are not.

Key quotation

words are very rascals
(Feste, Act 3, Scene 1)

It's not only characters within plays that draw attention to the folly of each other. Shakespeare's depiction of characters suggests an element of **satire** at work in *Twelfth Night*, as if he invites the audience to see the shortcomings of certain character types and concepts. In his depiction of Malvolio's joyless demeanour, it may be that wider criticism of Puritanism's austere values is implied. The same may be the case with the Petrarchan melancholy of Orsino.

> **satire** humour that pokes fun at people or situations in order to make (relatively) serious points or criticism

Comedy as a corrective

Although some characters choose to adopt foolish roles, Malvolio is made a fool of. One of the functions of comedy is to correct socially unacceptable behaviour: those characters who are the subject of mockery are publicly humiliated and encouraged to reflect on their actions and possibly amend them. In doing so, they become more in line with 'normal' behaviour.

The plotters and (usually) the audience see Malvolio's actions as going against the spirit of life (as they see it) and so the prank played upon him is an attempt to reveal his hypocrisy and then deflate his pomposity. For some, part of the fun is seeing a man who 'gets above himself' being brought down to earth.

Activity 7

How far do you agree with the following statements about the functions and types of comedy in *Twelfth Night*? Give reasons for your answer.

- Shakespeare uses Orsino as a way of satirizing the Petrarchan lover, poking fun at melancholy and excessive self-interest. The opening scene, rather than inviting sympathy, encourages you to laugh at Orsino's inflated sense of his own misery. Orsino therefore never really captures the audience's imagination. Instead, he is a figure of fun.

- Feste is the only character who doesn't succumb to the madness of love and grief. He stands to one side, offering witty comments, but he's also a sad figure, never quite fitting into the households he serves. His humour is also cutting, especially his barbed gloating to Malvolio in Act 5, Scene 1.

- Sir Toby and Sir Andrew are the most entertaining aspect of *Twelfth Night*. They are indecent and disrespectful, but their knockabout comic pairing is always destined to fail. Behind the clowning, there's a sinister edge.

Comic cruelty

In real life, the borderline between mockery and bullying is sometimes difficult to distinguish. Although mockery can be done with fondness, it can also be done to cause hurt. Ridiculing people and including them in laughter, even inviting self-deprecation, can be a way of sustaining relationships in real life. Humour can bond or divide. In *Twelfth Night*, the line between light-hearted mockery and a cruel variety of ridicule is not always clear-cut. Certain forms of humour such as wordplay don't require a target, but mockery and satire do.

Activity 8

Explore the manner in which Sir Toby mocks and tricks Sir Andrew. Consider:

- the exchange in Act 1, Scene 3 between Maria and Sir Toby before Sir Andrew arrives on stage, which begins **'That quaffing and drinking…'**. Notice the way he ironically defends Sir Andrew and the way he draws attention to his appearance

- the dialogue in Act 1, Scene 3 that begins **'Then hadst thou had an excellent head of hair'**. This again draws attention to Sir Andrew's appearance. Is it accurate to describe Sir Toby's encouragement of Sir Andrew's vain pursuit of Olivia as cruel?

- Sir Toby's mockery of his friend's dancing and lack of talent in the final 20 lines of Act 1, Scene 3. Is this merely fun?

- Sir Toby and Fabian's encouragement to Sir Andrew and stirring up of trouble from the start of Act 3, Scene 2 until Maria enters. Is this manipulative?

- how you react to Sir Toby's dismissal of his friend in Act 5, Scene 1. This will depend on how this scene is performed. Should these lines, spoken just before the knights leave the stage, be delivered comically or is there a cruelty in the way Sir Andrew is addressed?

Tips for assessment

Writing about the methods used by a dramatist is an essential aspect of your studies. When you explore the actions and words used by characters, consider how the dramatist shows these. The physical comedy in *Twelfth Night* complements the witty dialogue but is an important contrast to the darker humour that is also present. As you write, consider the different purposes of Shakespeare's comedy and how it adds to the success of the play.

Activity 9

One of the central debates about comedy and cruelty in the play centres on the treatment of Malvolio. You will explore this in more detail later, but for now consider the nature of his punishment. His humiliation is public and involves being made to look ridiculous in yellow stockings and then treated as a madman. Is this a hilarious type of comic torture or does this classify as cruelty? At which point, if any, does the laughter cease?

The treatment of Malvolio borders comedy and cruelty

The comedic ending

Tragedies end in death and comedies end in marriage. This simple distinction applies to *Twelfth Night* in part. Death is avoided (Sebastian emerges from his supposed watery grave) and Maria and Sir Toby marry. There is betrothal (rather than marriage) between the two central love pairings. Superficially, this seems like the happy ending that comedy leads us to expect. However, there are some less happy moments at the end of the play, which the audience might see as discordant, or jarring, rather than providing a complete sense of closure.

Activity 10

Look again at Act 5, Scene 1. Make a list of those events that might be deemed 'positive' or 'discordant'. Use a table like the one below to organize your thoughts.

Positive events	Discordant events
Sebastian and Viola are reunited	Malvolio threatens revenge

Comedy normally presents the audience with an ending that suggests the community has come together and any disagreements have been resolved. Comedic endings prefer community over the individual and, in some ways, the genre offers a pattern for productive society: one solves problems and constructs positive relationships. Unity, rather than isolation, is held up as a model for happiness.

Malvolio refuses to be part of the community at the end of *Twelfth Night*, however, preferring to maintain conflict rather than heal wounds. For some audiences, Malvolio can be dismissed as someone who simply can't take a joke. However, Olivia's view that he has been shabbily treated seems accurate too. In his essay, *Happy Endgames* (1990), Graham Holderness writes:

> Malvolio, bitterly disillusioned and (in Olivia's words) 'notoriously abus'd' [*Act 5, Scene 1*], has excluded himself from the compact of cheerfulness and gaiety secured by the rest of the cast. Possessed by vindictive rage, he unites both those who have fooled him and those to whom his own folly has been exposed, in a comprehensive passion of indignation: 'I'll be reveng'd on the whole pack of you!' [*Act 5, Scene 1*]. He places himself outside the newly integrated community of the play, and casts a shadow over its delicately achieved balance of concord and reconciliation [...] even in his absence, his painful alienation and his oath of vengeance brood ominously over the play's closure.

Activity 11

How do you respond to Graham Holderness's view? Does Malvolio's aggressive and wounded exit undermine the happiness of the play's ending?

Activity 12

You will explore Feste's closing song later in this book. In preparation, look closely at the lyrics of his song at the end of Act 5, Scene 1 and consider:

- how adulthood and society is presented in the second stanza
- how marriage is presented in the third stanza
- how old age is presented in the fourth stanza.

Activity 13

In the closing lines of the play, Feste acknowledges **'that's all one'** *(Act 5, Scene 1)*, suggesting that nothing really matters, and offers a song that reminds us that *'it raineth every day'*. What is the effect of closing the play in this downbeat way? If Feste is a wise fool who appears to see the wisdom and folly of man, do you agree that his pessimistic view of life is an accurate one, and that the froth of love and carousing are no antidote to the overriding problems of existence?

Is Feste a wise fool?

Writing about genre

Relating the play to its genre will help you to get away from simply writing about the events of the play or the actions of the characters. Dealing with *Twelfth Night* as part of a wider literary context, that of comedy, will help you to bring a sharper focus to the points you make. Studying the genre of comedy will illuminate your analysis of how Shakespeare uses and plays with conventions of the genre. It makes sense to have a working knowledge of the aspects of the genre that are found in a variety of comedic plays, but also to be alert to when writers challenge your expectations.

It is important to remember that writers don't write to a formula. Although you may be able to see the skeleton of the genre in *Twelfth Night*, when writing about the play as a comedy avoid the temptation simply to spot comedic elements and say 'and this is comedic'. Look beyond the feature and consider what it means. What does Viola's resourcefulness signify? What is distinctive about Malvolio's punishment? Could it be regarded as conventional?

Characterization and Roles

Some older critical approaches treat characters as if they are real people, and explore the beliefs and psychology of characters, as if they have a choice in what they do and say. While any study of character needs to start from what is done and said by the characters on stage, it's essential to explore them as *constructs*. The writer – in this case Shakespeare – decides everything in terms of what appears on the page. Writing about characters is insightful when it looks at *how* characters are constructed, rather than just describing their actions.

There is a difference in writing about characters and *characterization*. The latter looks at the choices made by the dramatist and thinks more widely about the character in relation to character type, role and function in the text. Stepping back and thinking about the choices made by the playwright is comparable to watching a film and thinking less about the things the characters do on screen, and more about what the director, scriptwriter, make-up artist, and so on decide to show. Drama is, of course, a special kind of text where different productions of plays can lend a different slant to a character. Make sure you balance what is on the page with how it might translate on stage.

Viola

As the protagonist of the comedy, Viola's **character arc** traces the journey from sadness to fulfilment. You have already explored how Viola occupies the role of the resourceful protagonist whose belief in good fortune helps her to progress. A straightforward reading of Viola may well see her as a buoyant, go-getting character who adopts a positive manner and rises above her worries.

There is some merit in this view: the idea that Viola embodies the irrepressible **romantic heroine** is supported by her depiction in Act 1, Scene 2, where her optimistic response to her situation and suspected loss contrasts with the dour, languid attitude of Orsino to his problems in the preceding scene.

> **character arc** the progress and development of a character during the text
>
> **romantic heroine** the central female character in a text centred on love; a character who overcomes the problems before her

In modern romantic comedy films, it is conventional for the protagonists to have attractive qualities: they are often physically appealing and have talents, skills or alluring qualities that engage both the audience and also other characters within the text. Shakespeare creates a heroine in Viola who possesses these traits; Malvolio acknowledges in Act 1, Scene 5 that Viola is **'very well-favoured'** and these traits are shown the first scene in which Viola appears.

Activity 1

Explore the attractive qualities of Viola in Act 1, Scene 2. Consider:

- her response to Sebastian's possible demise
- the mystery surrounding her background
- the compliment she offers the Captain
- the rapidity with which she devises a plan
- her talents
- her optimism.

Viola's appeal to both Orsino and Olivia is seen in the way Orsino lets her into his confidence and allows her a private audience in Act 1, Scene 5. A similar situation occurs with Olivia in the same scene where the countess dismisses her attendants and subsequently removes her veil. Viola possesses a power to beguile those of higher status than herself, and yet despite this, she is still subject to Orsino's command and attends to Olivia's beckoning. There is also a power in Viola's eloquence and determination, which allow her entry to see Olivia and also the ability to offer censure to her.

Key quotations

he hath known you but three days, and already you are no stranger.
(Valentine, Act 1, Scene 4)

yond young fellow swears he will speak with you
(Malvolio, Act 1, Scene 5)

The audience get an insight into Viola's emotions towards Orsino.

Activity 2

Explore the eloquence of Viola in Act 1, Scene 5. Consider:

- Malvolio's description of Viola's voice
- the balance between Viola's prepared speech and apparent off-the-cuff words
- the coded references to her disguised state
- her playful banter with Maria
- her persuasive qualities
- compliments and apparent condemnation
- the passion and poetry of her words
- her supposed anger.

Key quotations

I swear, I am not that I play
(Viola, Act 1, Scene 5)

I am no fee'd post, lady; keep your purse.
(Viola, Act 1, Scene 5)

It is possible to question this unerringly positive view of Viola. In *The Cambridge Introduction to Shakespeare's Comedies* (2008), Penny Gay makes the following points about the protagonist:

1. Viola's story takes place within the class-bound society […] as a page-boy, she loves the duke, and is in turn pursued by a titled lady […] Viola is extremely constrained in her behaviour and her public speech.

2. What, then, of the witty banter between unacknowledged lovers that we have come to expect in romantic comedies? Viola has only three scenes with Orsino – she has more with Olivia […] audiences might well wonder why Viola loves him.

3. In Viola's scenes with Olivia there is some word-play, but it has a curious air of desperation rather than delight.

4. Viola's final short soliloquy takes the audience back to what is arguably the deepest emotional connection in the play – her love for her lost brother.

Activity 3

What evidence can you find in the text to support Penny Gay's four points about Viola cited above? How far can it be argued that Viola's deepest love is for her brother?

catalyst in literary terms, a character or event that brings about change in others

Shakespeare presents Viola as a perceptive character who understands quickly the predicament she faces. There is a sense of self-awareness that she is trapped by her disguise and understands – through Olivia's response to her – how women can be taken in by men. It is possible to see Viola as having freedom and power in the play: she appears to move freely between the houses of Olivia and Orsino, and acts as a **catalyst** in the play. Yet comedy often flirts with tragic situations and the audience sees how Viola feels isolated by her predicament, calling herself **'poor monster'** *(Act 2, Scene 2)*. In dialogue with Orsino in Act 2, Scene 4, her inability to reveal her true self tips the balance towards pathos and suggests that her situation brings her pain rather than freedom.

It's also possible to see Viola as a lonely character: for most of the play she has nobody to confide in (aside from the audience) and is prevented from expressing her feelings publicly. She refers to her situation indirectly, either cryptically referencing her supposed sister or professing her love for Orsino in coded terms to Olivia in Act 1, Scene 5. Viola's last lines occur before the revelation of the Malvolio plot and, although she wishes for her **'maiden weeds'** *(Act 5, Scene 1)*, the audience never sees her attired in female clothing and Malvolio's imprisonment of the Captain prevents her acquisition of the clothes.

She may well declare **'I am Viola'** *(Act 5, Scene 1)*, but the man she will marry still refers to her as 'boy' and 'Cesario'. A certain sense of powerlessness can be seen in places: in Act 5, Scene 1 she states **'My lord would speak; my duty hushes me'** and later in the scene protests that she would happily die to please Orsino.

Activity 4

How do you respond to the following views of Viola? Which, if any, strike you as most convincing?

- Viola is a strong, determined female. Shakespeare draws attention to her pragmatism and strength of character. She bewitches the powerful and navigates a course through the difficult terrain of love. In depicting her ultimate success, Shakespeare celebrates the power of women to take charge of their own destiny and overcome life's problems.

- For all of Viola's attributes, she is, in the end, simply fortunate. She has the good luck to possess attractive qualities and relies on time to solve things rather than her own mettle. Shakespeare presents the reader with a protagonist on whom Fortune smiles: Sebastian's survival is the key to the play's ending, not Viola's resourcefulness.

- Viola is a tragic figure, isolated in Illyria and unhappy in her disguise as Cesario. She is, in practice, voiceless in that she can't express her thoughts freely. She exchanges any power she has when she pledges allegiance to Orsino, a man whose only quality seems to be his high status. She is left in limbo at the end of the play and fades into the background.

Key quotations

How easy is it for the proper false
In women's waxen hearts to set their forms!
(*Viola, Act 2, Scene 2*)

She sat like Patience on a monument,
Smiling at grief.
(*Viola, Act 2, Scene 4*)

Orsino

As the character with the opening lines in the play, Orsino's role at the centre of the love story seems clear. Yet in the middle of the play, Orsino seems to 'disappear': his role as the unrequited lover is established in the opening scene and then his problem is resolved without a great deal of effort on his part in Act 5, Scene 1. Although in some ways a flat character, Orsino can be read as a character who does change during the narrative.

As noted earlier, Orsino appears to be a version of the Petrarchan lover: the opening speech reveals a powerful but dissatisfied character, and this image seems to perpetuate throughout the play. Readers tend to attach negative descriptions to Orsino, yet in some performances he can appear charming.

Activity 5

Explore Orsino's words at the start of Act 1, Scene 1. Do you see him as poetic and gentle, or foppish and self-absorbed? Look closely at:

- the references to love, flowers and death
- the imperatives to the musicians
- the direct address to the spirit of love
- the knowing use of the pun on heart/hart
- the way he describes Olivia's attributes.

Activity 6

In Act 1, Scene 1, Orsino compares himself to Actaeon. Read the story of Actaeon and consider the following links between this myth and how Orsino perceives his own situation. Consider:

- the link between beauty, secrecy and cruelty
- the concept of desire leading to self-destruction
- issues of power and gender.

Does Orsino's comparison bear any relation to the situation between himself and Olivia as it appears in the play, or is he deluded and melodramatic?

Actaeon is ripped apart by his own hunting dogs; Diana and her women can be seen bathing on the other side of this waterfall in Italy

Actaeon

The myth of Actaeon is not precisely recorded but the central elements are as follows. Actaeon was a classical hero who, while hunting in the woods, saw Diana (the goddess of hunting) naked and bathing. The virgin goddess forbade him to speak. However, he called to his hunting dogs so Diana turned him into a deer. He ran from the dogs further into the wood but they pursued him and ripped him apart.

Orsino's varying instructions to the musicians in Act 1, Scene 1 seem to reveal his fickle nature: it's clearly not the music that changes, but his own feelings. Although Valentine assures Viola, as Cesario, in Act 1, Scene 5 that the duke is a man who is constant in his favours, Feste's pointed comment about Orsino's **'doublet of changeable taffeta'** *(Act 2, Scene 4)* seems more accurate. The comparison to an iridescent material that alters with the light suggests his changeability.

Feste also compares Orsino's mind to an opal, another entity whose colour alters with the light. Orsino's own statements seem contradictory in places, as if to suggest that he is subject to mood swings. In Act 1, Scene 4, he appears to have allowed the disguised Viola intimate access and has **'unclasp'd / To thee the book even of my secret soul'**, yet then declares that he prefers isolation. His views on men, women and love also appear to vary at times.

Activity 7

Explore Orsino's attitudes towards men, women and love as he expresses them in Act 1, Scene 4. Look closely at:

- his point about playfulness and constancy
- his admission about men's fancies
- his declaration about the depth and strength of men's feelings in comparison to those of women.

What apparent contradictions emerge in these statements and how might you explain them? Do they bring into question his feelings for Viola?

Key quotations

> I myself am best
> When least in company.
> *(Orsino, Act 1, Scene 4)*
>
> thy mind is a very opal
> *(Feste, Act 2, Scene 4)*
>
> Make no compare
> Between that love a woman can bear me
> And that I owe Olivia.
> *(Viola, Act 2, Scene 4)*

In many ways, Orsino seems foolish. His strident declaration of undying love for Olivia is clearly misplaced, as his allegiances change during the course of the play. A commonly held view is that Orsino is narcissistic: like the youth in Greek myth (see panel below), he appears to be more obsessed with himself and the depth of his feelings than any real feelings towards Olivia.

Narcissism

In classical mythology, Narcissus was a handsome, arrogant man who was tricked by a goddess and fell in love with his own reflection.

So far, much of what you have looked at paints a negative picture of Orsino. For some readers, he is illogical, fickle and petulant. Although these characters aren't real, it seems reasonable to ask what attracts Viola to Orsino, if such negative assessments are accurate. Yet as anyone who has fallen in love knows, sometimes love is blind, and we fall in love with people for undefinable reasons, perhaps even falling in love at first sight. It is possible to see the duke as a sentimental character, a man of emotion who wears his heart on his sleeve. He appreciates music, is commanding and yet has a gentle nature.

In Act 5, Scene 1, the audience is shown another aspect of Orsino's character, when he is presented with Antonio and recounts their previous meeting in **'the smoke of war'**. This speech casts Orsino in a heroic, active light, contrasting with the earlier images of his affected, passive self. The final scene suggests that the duke is less of a lovesick aristocrat than you might have assumed. His experience of battle and the rage he expresses when he feels he has been betrayed suggest a man of passion. He accuses Olivia of being uncivil and appears to threaten Viola. A sense of anger and cruelty emerges here.

By the end of the play, it is possible to argue that a more commanding and genuinely impassioned character has developed. Orsino's easy assumption of his status is seen in Act 5, Scene 1, when Malvolio exits and he commands Fabian to **'Pursue him, and entreat him to a peace'**, and Fabian does so.

Activity 8

Explore the way in which Orsino handles the arrival of Antonio in Act 5, Scene 1. Consider:

- the way he confers some glory on Antonio
- his dominance in the scene.

Activity 9

Are Orsino's threats serious? Explore his speech in Act 5, Scene 1, from **'Why should I not...'** to **'... within a dove'**, and consider whether Orsino is a credible threat. Is there a glimpse of potential tragedy at this point in the play?

Orsino's character arc seems to indicate uplift and the conventional comedic journey towards love. The nature of his feelings for Viola are worth exploring, as is the complexity of the ending, where he very quickly accepts Viola and overlooks his feelings for Olivia. His speech in Act 5, Scene 1, beginning **'Cesario, come...'** gives him the final word apparently, and although he is fully aware of Viola's true gender, he still insists on calling her Cesario until she is dressed in her female garb.

Orsino's reference to Viola as his **'fancy's queen'** *(Act 5, Scene 1)* perhaps suggests that her main appeal is as the indeterminately gendered character which first took his eye, rather than the woman he will marry. Structurally, Shakespeare allows Orsino space to demonstrate his newly found dominance when he commands the other characters in this scene, but this is followed by Feste's song, which gives a different impression of life, perhaps one at odds with the apparent joy.

> **Key quotation**
>
> Cesario, come –
> For so you shall be while you are a man.
> But when in other habits you are seen
> Orsino's mistress, and his fancy's queen.
> *(Orsino, Act 5, Scene 1)*

Activity 10

Consider the following views of Orsino. Which, if any, seem accurate to you?

- Orsino starts the play as a privileged, foppish and largely unsympathetic character who appears trapped in his self-made misery. Viola's entrance into his world shakes him from his stupor and reveals to the audience how love can alter people for good. The ending of the play gives the audience a fired-up, interesting and masculine duke and we begin to see why Viola is attracted to him.

- The duke we see in Act 1, Scene 1 is almost comic in his self-absorption, except that he is quite obviously a petulant and insular character for whom the audience feels little. This doesn't really change in spite of his burgeoning love for Viola and his heroics in the final scene. His cruelty emerges when he wields his power. As a romantic protagonist, he's a failure: the audience dislike him.

- Shakespeare spends most of the play subjecting Orsino to ridicule. The Petrarchan lover **archetype** is held up for mockery and, despite the masculine bravado and impassioned speeches, Orsino's repressed homosexuality is always present. Even his final speech suggests he prefers Viola as a boy, and his supposedly commanding last words are comically undercut by Feste's song. He's a fool rather than a hero.

archetype a typical example; the original pattern or model of something

Olivia

Olivia can be seen as a counterpart to Orsino in some ways: both are characters who wield social power in the world of Illyria and both commence the play as melancholic characters. Their journey in the play, like most comedic arcs, is one that ends in betrothal. Both are changed by their interaction with Viola and, on a superficial level at least, they appear to be changed and happier characters by the final scene of the play.

One of Shakespeare's structural choices is to allow the audience to hear about Olivia before she appears on stage. In the previous section, you saw how Orsino views Olivia as a cruel mistress, a version of the idealized Petrarchan love interest. Other characters also offer views on Olivia and her grief.

Activity 11

Explore the way other characters describe Olivia's manner in the following lines. What is the overriding impression created of Olivia by these words?

- Valentine's speech in Act 1, Scene 1, from **'So please my lord'** to **'her sad remembrance'**

- The Captain's six-line speech in Act 1, Scene 2, beginning **'A virtuous maid...'**

- Maria's first bit of dialogue in Act 1, Scene 3.

When Olivia finally appears on stage in Act 1, Scene 5, her initial interaction is with Feste, in which he suggests she is foolish for mourning her brother's death. Although a great deal depends upon performance, it might be that the Olivia the audience sees doesn't quite align with the views expressed by the other characters in earlier scenes. Rather than portray Olivia as the grief-stricken, frigid authoritarian that the audience are led to expect, some directors choose to present her as a skittish, playful and sexually frustrated countess.

Activity 12

In a later chapter you will explore the impact of performance choices upon interpretation, but at this point it would be useful to think about how you view Olivia in her initial interactions in Act 1, Scene 5, in particular:

- How seriously is the imperative **'Take the fool away'** delivered?

- How playful is her dialogue with Feste?

- She appears to act as referee between Feste and Malvolio. Where, if anywhere, do her sympathies lie?

One way of viewing Olivia is to see her as a female character who finds herself in a position of power after the deaths of her father and brother. Her role as female head of household appears challenged by some of the male inhabitants of the house: Feste has been absent without permission and Sir Toby is making a mockery of the decorum of the house with his carousing. Olivia appears to reject the world of the living, especially that of men, and retreats behind a veil. Her control (if that's how her manner can be described) is very quickly altered by the appearance of Viola in Act 1, Scene 5.

Activity 13

Explore the transformation of Olivia in Act 1, Scene 5. Pay close attention to:

- the possible reason(s) why Olivia chooses to admit Viola, from **'Of what personage...'** to **'Let him approach'**

- the curt responses Olivia gives to Viola such as **'a comfortable doctrine'** and **'it is heresy'**

- the removal of the veil. Why might Olivia choose to expose herself in this fashion at this point?

- her feelings towards Orsino during her speech from **'Your lord does know...'** to **'... answer long ago'**

- how an actor playing the part of Olivia might react during Viola's speech beginning **'Make me a willow cabin...'**, and how the line **'What is your parentage?'** might be delivered to show different emotions

- why Olivia asks about Viola's parentage

- the possible reasons Olivia is attracted to Viola. What are the **'youth's perfections'** and what is meant by **'Mine eye too great a flatterer for my mind'**? What does it reveal about Olivia?

Once Viola exits in Act 1, Scene 5, Olivia admits the rapidity with which she has fallen for Viola and, rather than trying to control matters (as she appears to want to do earlier in the scene), she seems to accept the uncertainty of the moment. In a short space of time, she is made dizzy by desire and throws off her veil. The seemingly powerful countess has succumbed to emotions beyond her control and philosophizes about the role of fate in shaping life.

Key quotation

Fate, show thy force; ourselves we do not owe.
What is decreed, must be: and be this so.
(*Olivia, Act 1, Scene 5*)

Olivia's awareness that she is acting out of character is expressed in Act 3, Scene 1. Prior to this, the audience sees her pretend that Viola has left her ring behind and risk looking foolish.

Olivia admits that she is at Viola's mercy and in her speech from 'Give me leave...' to '... due west' (*Act 3, Scene 1*), a range of images is used in which Olivia suggests her vulnerability. The image of bear-baiting is used, suggesting that the countess is, like a bear, tied to a stake by her vulnerability. Viola is cast in the role of an unmuzzled dog, tormenting and injuring her. This image recalls Orsino's earlier analogy of Actaeon and Diana. The outpouring of emotion sits in contrast with Olivia's earlier ice queen act. When the clock strikes during her speech, the audience notes a sense of jittery energy that has replaced the earlier guise of control.

Olivia's hurried betrothal in Act 4, Scene 3 (to Sebastian, although she thinks it's Viola) and her rapid, unquestioning response to the revelation of true identities in Act 5, Scene 1 (she says 'Most wonderful!') appear odd. Although a lot is explained by the fantastical and light nature of comedy, you might think how you react to Olivia's easy acceptance of a husband who she thought was somebody else and whether, in fact, this suggests that problems, rather than happiness, lie ahead for her.

Sir Mark Rylance played Olivia in an all-male performance of *Twelfth Night* at the Globe theatre in 2012

Have you not set mine honour at the stake,
And baited it with all th' unmuzzled thoughts
That tyrannous heart can think?
(Olivia, Act 3, Scene 1)

 Activity 14

How do you react to the following views of Olivia? What evidence in the text can you find to support these views?

- Olivia's story reveals how the powerful are affected by love just like any other character. The giddiness and vulnerability Olivia shows make the audience warm to the character. It is clear that her melancholy was just a front, and the arrival of Viola releases her from the role of austere countess. Her partnership with Sebastian is a fitting end to her story and suggests that she has found joy.

- Olivia is a fool. Her grief is just posturing, her attempts to control her household fail, and she acts like a lovesick teenager, attaching herself to Viola based on physical attraction. Her story confirms that the powerful are, in fact, idiotic and unable to control themselves. Her acceptance of Sebastian – who she barely knows – confirms her weakness and suggests that problems loom.

Sebastian and Antonio

Although a less central character, Sebastian is key to the resolution of the play. He only appears in a handful of scenes and, although there are glimpses of his personality – his determination to head to Orsino's court without Antonio, his willingness to fight, and his befuddled but positive reaction to Olivia – his importance is mainly structural. His resemblance to Viola is essential for the confusions over love and comic violence that arise, and his survival and arrival at Orsino's court allows the pairs of lovers to find each other.

Antonio is left out in the cold at the end of the play. It's possible to see him as the most honest and brave character in the text. He follows Sebastian despite personal risk and openly declares his feelings in Act 2, Scene 2. As you saw in the chapter on context, the issue of the precise nature of his feelings towards Sebastian can lead to some interesting production choices. As you study the nature of this relationship, consider why Shakespeare chooses to leave Antonio unpartnered at the end of the play.

Key quotations

The gentleness of all the gods go with thee!
(Antonio, Act 2, Scene 1)

I do adore thee so
Antonio, Act 2, Scene 1)

Activity 15

How do you react to the following views? Is it possible to argue against them?

- Sebastian's only importance is his resemblance to his sister. He has no significant character traits: his function is merely structural.

- Sebastian's attitude towards Antonio is dismissive. He appears to treat Sebastian coolly. The audience, like Sebastian, don't really care much for Antonio.

- Sebastian's main love is for his sister: his relationship with Olivia is an afterthought. The audience are more satisfied at the reuniting of the twins than the marriages.

- Shakespeare plays with the homoerotic elements of Sebastian and Antonio's relationship, but then returns us to the 'normality' of heterosexual pairings at the end of the play.

Feste

In the previous chapter you considered Feste's role as an allowed fool and explored the licence he enjoys to offer witty, critical comments to those in authority. Later in this book you will explore his use of language and song. For now, consider his structural contribution to the play. In Trevor Nunn's 1996 film adaptation of the play, Feste (played by Ben Kingsley) seems to occupy the role of overseer: he appears at the start and acts as narrator, clearly aware that Viola is in disguise. The film's closing shots show him wandering off along the coast, a free spirit who appears to see life's wider patterns.

In some readings of the play, Feste almost stands outside the action of the play, not orchestrating events but offering comment, as if he is the bridge between the characters and the audience. Feste might be said to have a **choric** function in the play, summarizing, criticizing and drawing attention to the actions of others. He is given the closing lines in the play, his lyrics offering a melancholic contrast to the apparent harmony of marriage.

In some ways, Feste might be seen as a nonchalant observer who sits above the madness of love, yet his coolness and distant wit seem to become more biting in his interactions with Malvolio, a character who appears to stand in direct opposition to the improvising, freewheeling persona of the clown. There appears to be a sense of **schadenfreude** about Feste's lines in Act 5, Scene 1 towards Malvolio and perhaps a cruel joy in his baiting of the steward in the dark room scene. As you study Feste, consider the balance between wit, levity (a light-hearted approach to serious issues), melancholy and bitterness in his words.

Key quotation

And thus the whirligig of time brings in his revenges.
(Feste, Act 5, Scene 1)

choric performing the role of chorus, a term derived from Greek tragedy where a group of actors standing aside from the action of the play offer collective comment on events

schadenfreude the cruel pleasure taken from the downfall of others

Activity 16

Explore Feste's interactions with Maria, Viola, Orsino, Olivia, Malvolio, Sir Toby and Sir Andrew. Does he always act as a detached observer and sarcastic critic?

You could use a table like the one below to record your notes.

Character and reference	Quotation	Analysis
Maria Act I, Scene 5	Feste: Let her hang me; he that is well hanged in this world needs to fear no colours	Feste is responding to Maria's assertion that Olivia will be displeased. He appears disinterested and uses puns – a sexual one on 'well hanged' and one blending collars (hanging) and colours (flags). He appears self-assured and uses language in a playful way to deflect criticism.

Malvolio

Your response to Malvolio depends very much on performance and the extent to which you see him as a pompous, hypocritical character who deserves everything he gets, or whether he is a conscientious, if dour, steward who – like so many of the characters – is deluded about love. In earlier sections, you explored his role as the antithesis to Feste. His initial entrance might be played to emphasize his killjoy puritanical qualities – a wet blanket who spoils the final fling of twelfth night. Yet by the end of the play he may well attract your sympathy. The issue of comic cruelty you explored earlier is relevant here: To what extent is Malvolio's punishment greater than his 'crime'?

In some ways, Malvolio is a hypocrite. The joy and scorn he pours on the livelier elements of human conduct is seen in his own fantasies in Act 2, Scene 5. At this point in the play, he believes Olivia is in love with him, and he gives free rein to his hopes about what his future with her might involve.

Key quotation

I thank my stars, I am happy!
(Malvolio, Act 2, Scene 5)

Activity 17

Look closely at Malvolio's fantasies in Act 2, Scene 5. Do they make you laugh or do you see him as a hypocritical character who incites your dislike? Consider:

- how he views his apparel and imagined sexual relationship
- how he sees his relationship with Sir Toby
- his joy at his mistaken interpretation of the letter
- whether you feel sorry for Malvolio, given the joy he feels.

Sir Toby, Sir Andrew and Maria

You have explored the knights' roles as fools in the previous chapter and looked at how their antics echo the classic comedy double act. Yet there is also a darker aspect to their relationship, in which Sir Toby may well be seen as manipulating his friend. While Sir Toby's profligate character usually entertains audiences, there is the potential to feel sympathy for Sir Andrew, who appears to believe that Olivia may be interested in him and suggests that he was dear to someone in his past. The two knights are mainly used for comic business, and the physical qualities of the double act come through in the dancing and comic violence in the plot. Whether there is a melancholy in their behaviour and actions is worth your consideration.

Although a minor character, Maria's role in orchestrating the plot against Malvolio is important to the meanings of the play. Comedy often celebrates the rebelliousness of servants: Maria's daring and creativity in designing the plot reminds the reader that although the powerful people of Illyria hold sway socially, the streetwise servant is more than capable of wielding their own type of power. Maria begins the play as a gentlewoman who is governed by her superiors, but ends up married to a knight. Her actions suggest that feistiness can bring success.

Feisty Maria is a good match for Sir Toby.

Key quotations

I was adored once too.
(Sir Andrew, Act 2, Scene 3)

... on that vice in him will my revenge find notable cause to work.
(Maria, Act 2, Scene 3)

 Activity 18

To what extent do you agree with the following statements?

- Sir Toby is a layabout who confirms the general stereotype of the work-shy, privileged upper classes.

- Sir Andrew is a character who elicits sympathy. Although a coward and a fool, there is something sad about him.

- The audience laughs when the knights receive their wounded heads. There is no sense in which we feel sympathy at this point.

- The rapid marriage of Sir Toby and Maria, and the isolation of Sir Andrew is of little interest to the audience.

- Maria is a version of Viola: both woman are positive, creative forces who secure the love of powerful men.

- Although playful, Maria is also nasty and cruel. She manipulates Sir Toby's affections to acquire herself some status.

Writing about characterization and roles

Thinking about characters in relation to their functions in the narrative will help you to see the way in which their stories contribute to the design of the play as a whole. Be alert for parallels between characters, especially the way in which the actions and words of characters are echoed by another. Look carefully at how characters appear to be archetypes, but also how the playwright gives them complexity, making them rounded rather than one-dimensional.

Try to write about characters in relation to dramatic method. Explore, for example, who is given the lion's share of the dialogue and at which points in the narrative. Think about the character's journey in the story and where they end up. Consider which characters gain the audience's sympathies and why. Which actions invite you to understand their joy? Are you, as the audience, in possession of more information about the character than they are? Draw together these elements and then conclude how they function within the play.

Twelfth Night is a play in which language is central. While this seems obvious (after all, any text requires language to make meaning), *Twelfth Night* focuses at times on the instability of language itself. In the play, words are used for wooing, commanding and teasing. Words are used to wound, to jest and to propose.

The language of courtly love

You have already considered the way in which Orsino's overblown words about his apparent love for Olivia in Act 1, Scene 1 are held up for ridicule. The conventions of Petrarchan love poetry and courtly love were well established by the time Shakespeare wrote *Twelfth Night* and, in Orsino's dialogue, Shakespeare offers the audience a **parody** of the language of courtly love. In imitating its emotional intensity, its meaningless is revealed.

The imagery in Orsino's words also echoes another subgenre of poetry, that of *carpe diem*. This text type, often written by a male, was a type of poem in which the poet/speaker addressed his lover, urging her to hurry up with the business of lovemaking before her physical attractiveness waned. Orsino's speech contains elements of this style, linking ideas of love to death and time.

The Sonnets, a collection of poems written by Shakespeare and published in 1609, plays with courtly love and *carpe diem* ideas. *The Sonnets* contain **anti-Petrarchan** elements, which seem oppositional to classic love poetry. 'Sonnet 130' presents a mistress who is definitely not the stereotypical goddess:

> My mistress' eyes are nothing like the sun;
>
> Coral is far more red than her lips' red;
>
> If snow be white, why then her breasts are dun;
>
> If hairs be wires, black wires grow on her head.

The opening four lines above show a deliberate attempt to suggest that 'real' women are very unlike the way some poets present them. Implicit in this is a playful criticism and ridicule of the sappy love poet. Orsino's words are treated in the same manner: the audience is invited to see the superficial way he regards love and Olivia. His dialogue contains **cliché** and **hyperbole**, which reveal the hollowness of his speech. Orsino's words (and the ones he gives Viola to speak to Olivia) seem flat and rehearsed.

Key quotation

Methought she purg'd the air of pestilence
(Orsino, Act 1, Scene 1)

Activity 1

Explore Orsino's initial speech in Act 1, Scene 1 again, this time looking more closely at how elements of language contribute to the mood of the speech. Consider the use of **imperative**, **exclamatory**, **apostrophe**, **aural images**, **visual images** and **tactile images**. Notice how the overuse of dramatic speech and **rhetorical devices** draws attention to the emotional nature of the words.

Activity 2

Now explore Orsino's dialogue in Act 5, Scene 1 from **'What, to perverseness?'** to **'.... henceforth may never meet'**. Do these words seem as hollow as those spoken in the first scene? Why/why not?

anti-Petrarchan an attitude in some writing that deliberately presents a lover in 'realistic' rather than idealized ways

apostrophe a direct address to a third party, sometimes an inanimate object

aural image image that appeals to the sense of hearing

blazon originally a coat of arms or a shield on which pictures representing the family were depicted; by extension, a poem that provides a list of the attributes of a lover

carpe diem a latin term meaning 'seize the day' and, by extension, a poem or text type in which a would-be lover urges his mistress to make the most of time

cliché a phrase so overused and familiar that it appears stale

exclamatory an often dramatic phrase ending with an exclamation mark

hyperbole a type of exaggeration

imperative a command or order

parody an imitation of a person or genre for comic purposes

rhetorical devices language techniques that attempt to persuade

tactile image image that appeals to the sense of touch

visual image image that appeals to the sense of sight

Blazon

A **blazon** is a poem that gives a list of the qualities of a female lover, breaking her physical appearance down and often offering comment on them. A blazon was usually written by a male and addressed to a third party (by implication another male), in effect bragging about his lover's beauty.

In *Twelfth Night*, Olivia offers her own sarcastic blazon when Viola requests that she remove her veil. When Viola uses the conventional *carpe diem* sentiment that Olivia must procreate and preserve her beauty, Olivia retorts:

> **I will give out divers schedules of my beauty. It shall be inventoried, and every particle and utensil labelled to my will. As Item: two lips indifferent red; Item: two grey eyes, with lids to them; Item: one neck, one chin, and so forth. Were you sent hither to praise me?**
> *(Act 1, Scene 5)*

It seems that she is tired of the rehearsed speeches of Orsino's messengers and ridicules herself as a way of suggesting the vacuity of his clichéd love offerings. Oddly enough, once Olivia has fallen for Viola, she remarks:

> **Thy tongue, thy face, thy limbs, actions and spirit**
> **Do give thee five-fold blazon.**
> *(Act 1, Scene 5)*

While Orsino proclaims his love for Olivia, disguised Viola is unable to state her love for him openly

It appears that once the madness of true love strikes, Olivia finds herself sincerely uttering the very language she scoffs at. Perhaps Shakespeare ironizes the madness of love, fondly mocking how the very thing we see as tired and clichéd suddenly takes on fresh meaning when we fall in love.

Later in the play, Maria promises that in her forged letter she will write within the conventions of the blazon to taunt Malvolio. Her words, supposedly from Olivia, will draw attention to:

> **… the colour of his beard, the shape of his leg, the manner of his gait, the expressure of his eye, forehead and complexion…**
> *(Act 2, Scene 3)*

In *Twelfth Night*, the blazon becomes the property of the female rather than the male, as if Shakespeare is alerting you not only to the staleness of the blazon, but also to its gender bias. In the voices of the female characters, it becomes a form of power: Olivia uses it sarcastically and then spontaneously, and Maria uses it to deflate Malvolio. The blazon, a conventionally male form, is used as a tool by females to mock male pretensions.

Activity 3

Consider the idea that expressions of romantic love are always mocked in the play. Does *Twelfth Night* poke fun at outpourings of emotion?

simile a comparison between entities using the words 'like' or 'as'

trope a metaphorical use of language; from Greek, meaning 'to turn', i.e. where one thing is turned into another

Poetic language

You have considered how the language of courtly love is satirized in some parts of the play, yet the play contains some beautiful, affecting scenes where words capture the intensity of true emotion. In Act 1, Scene 5, Viola arrives and offers a prepared speech to Olivia, which she has **'taken great pains to con'**. The tired *carpe diem* phrases from **'Tis beauty truly blent...'** to **'leave the world no copy'** *(Act 1, Scene 5)* have little effect on Olivia. The change in her feelings, and perhaps the point where Olivia falls for Viola comes in the speech beginning **'If I did love you...'** *(Act 1, Scene 5)*, where Viola appears to speak sincerely about the lengths she would go to to win the heart of a lover. There is a great irony here, because Viola clearly has Orsino in mind as she speaks about love.

> ## Activity 4
>
> Explore the language of Viola's nine-line speech in Act 1, Scene 5 from **'Make me a willow cabin...'**. Consider the use of images related to nature, aural images, and Petrarchan love conventions. Is this a sincere example of how the words of love poetry can be captivating, or is there still a sense of hollowness and cliché?

> ## Activity 5
>
> Explore Olivia's nine-line speech to Viola in Act 3, Scene 1, starting **'Why then methinks...'**. To what extent do these words rely on conventional images of love? Are they heartfelt or predictable? Consider the use of images connected with animals and agriculture.

Metaphor and simile

Poetic language frequently makes use of **tropes** such as metaphor and **simile** as a way of expressing ideas through comparison. Consider Viola's speech where she talks of her 'sister' (that is, herself):

> **She never told her love**
> **But let concealment, like a worm i' th' bud**
> **Feed on her damask cheek.**
> *(Act 2, Scene 4)*

As ever, simply spotting features is of little use, so one way to make your analysis productive is to link language features to wider ideas and meanings in the play. In this speech, Viola is expressing how the inability to state your true feelings causes harm, and the comparisons focus on hidden entities.

The simile that compares the concealment of feelings to **'a worm i' th' bud'** *(Act 2, Scene 4)* revolves around natural imagery with the corruption of a potentially beautiful object – a bud – by another natural entity. Worms in this context seem insidious and penetrative. The comparison is extended to describe the worm of concealment eating away at the beauty of the female face (itself compared to a blended rose). You might consider further the sexual aspect of the simile, with the worm perhaps operating as a **phallic symbol**; as a comparison, explore William Blake's 'The Sick Rose', which employs similar allusions.

Taken together, the image created by the simile seems fairly horrific. It expresses the damage cause by desire when it is internalized. It would seem that Viola feels her emerging womanhood is being destroyed by the cruelty of being in love and being unable to pursue those feelings openly. Clearly, the wider themes of disguise, pain and love are embodied in the simile.

phallic symbol an object that represents or symbolizes the penis

Activity 6

Write a paragraph explaining the use of simile (and other language features) in the following quotation. Link your observations to the wider ideas of the play.

> She pin'd in thought,
> And with a green and yellow melancholy
> She sat like Patience on a monument,
> Smiling at grief.
> (Act 2, Scene 4)

Activity 7

Explore the use of metaphor and simile in *Twelfth Night*, remembering that metaphor isn't restricted to elevated poetic moments; for instance, Feste's observation that Orsino is an **'opal'** (Act 2, Scene 4) is satirical in nature, and Maria's comparison of her breasts to a **'buttery bar'** (Act 1, Scene 3) is comically coarse.

What do you notice about the type of comparisons made? Other than natural elements, what other entities are referred to?

Dramatic irony

Dramatic irony is used extensively in *Twelfth Night*, with the audience often holding superior knowledge to the characters on stage. An obvious example of this is the fact that Viola's true identity is known to the audience and not the characters. This leads to some comic moments, but also some touching ones. In the section above, you saw how Viola's 'willow cabin' speech was really inspired by her feelings for Orsino.

There is something comic about this, as Olivia mistakes these feelings of passion, but perhaps there is a kind of pathos here in that Viola is unable to state her love openly.

Activity 8

What different effects are created by the use of dramatic irony in the play? Make a list of examples of this technique and analyse the effects created.

You could use a table like the one below to record your findings.

Example of dramatic irony	Analysis
The audience is aware that Sebastian is alive by the start of Act 2, but Viola doesn't realize this until the final scene.	This suggests to the audience that a happy ending is likely and indicates that the growing complications of the love triangle will be resolved. In some ways, any tension created is dispelled by the knowledge that Sebastian's survival offers a way out of the play's problems.

Imagery

In the speeches you have looked at so far, you will have noticed that many of the images are drawn from recurring groups, such as the animal kingdom. In Orsino's speech in Act 1, Scene 1, reference is made to music, food, flowers and the sea. Imagery is one way of binding a play together, reinforcing some of the themes and helping to create mood. In his article *The Old Man and the Sea*, Royal Shakespeare Company (RSC) Associate Director David Farr has this to say about sea imagery in the play:

> [I] am constantly drawn back to my favorite metaphor in Shakespeare – the sea storm as redemptive force.
>
> O if it prove,
> Tempests are kind and salt waves fresh in love!
> (Viola, *Twelfth Night,* Act 3, Scene 4)
>
> What these plays all need, in production, is that sensitivity to the sea. They need a strange, elusive poetry that renders fortune, fate, chance (all words constantly used in these plays) as agents of a greater power. That makes the sea both God and Devil, and that makes man tiny and vulnerable [...] But we are not just overwhelmed by the ocean, we also contain it. Orsino in *Twelfth Night* describes his passion as 'all as hungry as the sea' *(Act 2, Scene 4)*. The human soul is an ocean tossed by storms of passion, deep and bottomless in its need for succor and nourishment. Storm is a metaphor for our own desires.

Activity 9

How do you react to the following questions arising from Farr's article?

- Is the sea storm in *Twelfth Night* really a force of redemption? Does the natural event actually begin the process of bringing the lovers together?
- Does the play celebrate the power of the sea over man?
- In what way can the storm that separates Viola and Sebastian be seen as a metaphor for human desire?

Key quotations

I'll sacrifice the lamb that I do love,
To spite a raven's heart within a dove.
(Orsino, Act 5, Scene 1)

O thou dissembling cub! What wilt thou be
When time has sow'd a grizzle on thy case?
(Orsino, Act 5, Scene 1)

Playing with language

Comic language makes great use of puns and playful use of words, occasionally for the purposes of bawdy humour. Rude jokes often revolve around innuendo or **double entendre** and a version of this wordplay is found in Act 1, Scene 4 where Orsino offers a kind of blazon about Viola, praising her rubious lip and commenting that her **'small pipe / Is as the maiden's organ'**. Here the pun is based upon references to male genitalia and the joke works because Viola is a woman dressed as man, and originally would have been played by a young man.

> **double entendre** a phrase with a double meaning, often a risqué one

Activity 10

Complete a table with some of the examples of puns and double entendres in *Twelfth Night*. Try to explain the nature of the joke in the context of the play.

Example of wordplay	Analysis
MARIA: ... I pray you bring your hand to th' buttery bar and let it drink.	Maria is teasing Sir Andrew. Bawdy language suggests physical aspects – in performance this is often accompanied by physical humour to bring out the risqué joke. The joke about consumption ('let it drink') has sexual connotations.

Puns and jokes play with language and deliberately confuse meanings: comedic language bristles with double meanings, verbal humour, misinterpretation and nonsensical words. Feste's notion that words are 'very rascals' (Act 3, Scene 1) suggests language's slipperiness and resistance to stable definition.

Some of the comic corruptions of language and ideas occur in the subplot, where Sir Toby's playful, non-compliant character gives rise to deliberate twisting of words and apparently invented language. His interaction in Act 1, Scene 3 with the woman who will become his wife is one where he deliberately misinterprets the meaning of 'confine' and thereby refuses Maria's scolding:

> MARIA: Ay, but you must confine yourself within the modest limits of order.
> SIR TOBY: Confine? I'll confine myself no finer than I am. These clothes are good enough to drink in...
> (Act 1, Scene 3)

The more nonsensical wordplay occurs where the three revellers – Sir Toby, Sir Andrew and Feste – carouse in Act 2, Scene 3 prior to the entrance of Malvolio. The sense that language can be rebellious, playful and defy logic appears to mirror the behaviour of the characters, as seen in this ridiculous exchange:

> SIR ANDREW: In sooth, thou wast in very gracious fooling last night, when thou spok'st of Pigrogromitus, of the Vapians passing the equinoctial of Queubus. 'Twas very good, i'faith. I sent thee sixpence for thy leman: hadst it?
> FESTE: I did impeticos thy gratillity: for Malvolio's nose is no whipstock, my lady has a white hand, and the Myrmidons are no bottle-ale houses.
> (Act 2, Scene 3)

The names here are invented (with the exception of the steward's) and the feeling is one of the festive surreality of revellers' conversations. The concept that language can be played with is also captured in Feste's 'chev'ril glove' image in Act 3, Scene 1, which suggests that words, like gloves, can be turned inside out. Some lines later, Feste acknowledges his own role as corrupter of language. Feste's conversation with Viola in Act 3, Scene 1 is riddling and the fool draws Viola into wordplay, allowing her to see that his riddles do contain wisdom.

Key quotations

A sentence is but a chev'ril glove to good wit – how quickly the wrong side may be turned outward!
(Feste, Act 3, Scene 1)

I am indeed not her fool, but her corrupter of words.
(Feste, Act 3, Scene 1)

This fellow is wise enough to play the fool,
And to do that well, craves a kind of wit
(Viola, Act 3, Scene 1)

Activity 11

Given Viola's acknowledgement of the wisdom in Feste's playful words, explore the meaning(s) of his statements in Act 3, Scene 1. Consider:

- his point about the contradictory nature of language
- his observations about husbands and fools
- the implication about facial hair.

Song

Music plays a significant part in *Twelfth Night*: it is featured in the opening lines of the play, is part of the rebellious behaviour in Act 2, Scene 3, and also ends the play. Feste's songs have important structural and linguistic functions in the text. His first contribution to the music of the play occurs at Act 2, Scene 3, when he responds to the knights' request for a love song. The lyrics of the song seem conventional, telling the story of a narrator who implores his mistress to cease roaming and meet her true love: *'Trip no further pretty sweeting: / Journeys end in lovers meeting'*.

Here the words echo the narrative of comedy: the idea that some sort of physical and metaphorical journey results in happiness, or that love is seen in the play itself when both Viola and Sebastian's journeys lead them to betrothal. The images and narrative of this song, unlike Feste's riddling prose, seem clear and direct. There is an obvious discrepancy between the creative, surreal Feste of Act 2, Scene 3 and the lyrics he sings, which have the sense of medieval love poetry. His second song, a few lines later, is less joyful. Feste's third and fourth songs are also melancholic. His final song forms the last words the audience hears. It is worth considering why Shakespeare ends the play with this downbeat account.

Feste's songs get progressively more melancholic as the play moves on

Activity 12

Read the lyrics to Feste's song in Act 2, Scene 3, which begins *'What is love?'* and consider the following responses to his words. Which, if any, do you agree with?

- This is another conventional and clichéd song, which uses the sentiments of *carpe diem* poetry. It's essentially meaningless and trite.

- There is some pathos in the song, especially for its onstage audience – two old men whose attractiveness to young women has passed.

- The song is at odds with comedy, which celebrates youth and love. The song introduces an uncomfortable edge to the scene and play.

Activity 13

Feste's song in Act 2, Scene 4 contains a range of gruesome images. Make a list of ideas in this song connected with death and explore Orsino's attitudes to it. Is it really 'silly sooth'?

Activity 14

How far do you agree with Paul Oliver's view of Feste's final song printed below? Is the song 'painful and disturbing' in the context of the play?

> The final song [...] pushes the triteness several steps further. The cliché of its structure as it runs through the various stages of the speaker's life, and the repetition of the fourth line asserting the essential greyness of life, threaten to impair the impact badly. But how different is the song's effect in the theatre! The context (the ending of the play, the exit of the newly matched couples, the sense that Feste is shut out from the general happiness, being a visitor to both households but an inmate of neither) contrives to make the play end on a note which is at least as much painful and disturbing as celebratory.

Writing about language

When you write about language, never do it in isolation. You will not say much by simply spotting features. Instead, points about language should be linked closely to ideas about meaning and character. This section has focused on the larger features of language such as imagery and patterns and what they reveal about the ideas in the play. There may be times when exploring the connotations of single words is useful because it illuminates an aspect of character. Be wary of learning too many complex and little-used terms, as they may not help you write well about the way language is used in the text.

Themes

Themes help to unify a story. They often explore moral ideas – concepts that seem applicable to the lives of most people. Concepts such as love are prevalent in *Twelfth Night*, and are explored through the actions of different characters and scenes. They invite us to see the text as having a kind of unity of design – an ordered, shaped message that comes to represent what is 'meant' by *Twelfth Night*. In seeing thematic ideas played and replayed during the course of the play, the audience come to see what they consider to be 'the point' of the story. As with character and performance, themes can be interpreted in various ways and can provoke a range of readings.

Love

Comedies focus on the process of achieving happiness and this often comes in the form of love. The story arc of *Twelfth Night* shows how characters who appear unhappy at the start of the play – either through loss or unrequited love – achieve happiness by the resolution of the narrative. The play reveals different types of love, often satirizing the pretensions of self-love such as those exhibited by Orsino and Malvolio. The Petrarchan idealizing of love is also held up for ridicule, but the play does show how love and lust can rejuvenate and make anybody, regardless of rank and status, act emotionally.

Activity 1

a) Consider the references to love in these lines from Act 1. Who speaks these lines and in what context? What is revealed about love and desire?

- **my desires, like fell and cruel hounds, / E'er since pursue me** *(Act 1, Scene 1)*
- **all this to season / A brother's dead love, which she would keep fresh** *(Act 1, Scene 1)*
- **Love-thoughts lie rich when canopied with bowers.** *(Act 1, Scene 1)*
- **for whose dear love / (They say) she hath abjur'd the company / And sight of men** *(Act 1, Scene 2)*
- **you call in question the continuance of his love.** *(Act 1, Scene 4)*
- **a barful strife! / Whoe'er I woo, myself would be his wife.** *(Act 1, Scene 4)*
- **If I did love you in my master's flame, / With such a suff'ring, such a deadly life, / In your denial I would find no sense** *(Act 1, Scene 5)*
- **Write loyal cantons of contemned love** *(Act 1, Scene 5)*
- **Love make his heart of flint that you shall love** *(Act 1, Scene 5)*
- **Even so quickly may one catch the plague?** *(Act 1, Scene 5)*

b) Make your own list of quotations referring to love from Acts 2 to 5 and consider what is revealed about this theme. Is love always associated with joy?

You have already seen how Orsino's narcissistic love is satirized in the first scene. Whether his later feelings towards Viola are genuine is debatable. Often on stage, their physical attraction is played out in looks and other non-verbal action: some performances suggest that a deep bond is present and that the removal of her disguise legitimizes his uncomfortable homoerotic feelings. The nature of their love (or certainly his feelings) is hard to gauge. It's possible to argue that Orsino's union with Viola is an afterthought: even in the final scene, he seems to focus on Olivia as a love object and only accepts Viola when it becomes clear that Olivia will marry Sebastian.

Activity 2

Read Larry Champion's views below on Orsino's mood shifts in Act 5, Scene 1. What is being implied about Orsino's choices at the end of the play and, by extension, the nature of his relationship with Viola? Do you agree with Champion's views?

 [Within] the space of a few short lines his unbounded love has been exploded by an equally unbounded temper. The second shift is even more revelatory of the true quality of his love. When Olivia's husband is produced, Orsino, at the point of being outfaced altogether, determines to 'share in this most happy wreck' by receiving the love which Viola has for some time been anxious to offer.

When genuine attraction strikes the other characters, love appears to act as a catalyst – it brings about extraordinary changes in mood. Olivia changes from an icy, grieving sister into a skittish, excitable young woman. She removes her veil, devises a way to make Viola return and admits how love's plague can so quickly take hold. It seems that Shakespeare reveals the power of love as an emotional response: it enlivens the countess, but it's also a process full of doubt for Olivia, as Larry Champion remarks:

 [She] is not without moments of remorse as she realizes the indignity of her actions. For instance, in Scene i she tells Cesario not to be afraid, that she will pursue no further (141, 143), and in Scene iv she laments that there is 'something in me that reproves my fault' (223). She is unable to contain her love, however, and at another point openly declares her affection so strong that 'Nor wit nor reason can my passion hide' (III,i,164). Moreover, a short time later she becomes ridiculously flustered at Cesario's very approach.

The dawning of love prompts Olivia to remove her veil and find a way to make Viola return.

Activity 3

Make a list of the characters who express feelings of love. Consider what is being shown about love and desire through the characters' actions.

Character	Actions relating to the theme of love and their significance
Viola	Viola's love for Orsino occurs rapidly, yet the source of her attraction to Orsino remains a mystery and seems unusual to the audience given the duke's foppishness. Her feelings cause her some pain ('a barful strife'), yet she remains constant in her affections and even woos Olivia on his behalf without complaint. Viola's love has to remain hidden from the other characters (but not the audience). Her love is selfless – she is prepared to die when Orsino threatens her and accedes to his rule at the end of the play. The other aspect to her love is her bond with Sebastian, another selfless attachment she never gives up on.

The pain wrought by love or unrequited love is explored in the play, and you might get the impression that rather than celebrating love, the play calls into question the simplistic notion that love solves everything, a notion that comedy conventionally suggests. For instance, Viola's feelings are painful, as she suggests in her speech in Act 2, Scene 4 where she describes how her 'sister' (that is, her) was eaten away by the misery that her unspoken love brought.

For Malvolio, there is no happy ending. His love for Olivia is a delusion and for a while it makes him happy. The truth is that it's a charade. For Antonio, his love for Sebastian, which is unfailingly selfless, goes unrewarded. Orsino's temporary anger in Act 5, Scene 1 over Viola's supposed betrayal nearly spills over into violence. Sir Andrew leaves the stage with a bloody head and no wife.

Although this is drama and not real life, it's easy to see how the speed of the betrothals at the end of the play strikes a note of caution. Just how suited are the marriage partners? Olivia is to marry Sebastian, a man she doesn't know and Orsino has quickly switched allegiance from Olivia, who he considered his ideal woman, to Viola who, for the time he's known her has been dressed as a boy. If this were real life, it would appear folly, but the play is operating in the realm of comedy, where rapid resolutions and love's madness is revealed.

> **Key quotation**
>
> She pin'd in thought,
> And with a green and yellow melancholy
> She sat like Patience on a monument,
> Smiling at grief.
> (Act 2, Scene 4)

Tips for assessment

Understanding how the themes of *Twelfth Night* interlink is important. It would be difficult to answer a question considering the presentation of love, for example, if you were not also familiar with its links to desire and sexuality – and the overriding theme of deception.

Desire and sexuality

Closely linked to the theme of love is that of sexuality. Comedy has long made jokes out of the bizarre actions that libido-driven characters perpetrate. Human desire is explored in the play and shown to be not only a source of humour, but also something to be positively celebrated. Olivia's initial attraction to Viola seems driven by lust. Sir Toby's relationship with Maria is often played on stage as a passionate attraction between two livewires.

Twelfth Night clearly invites the audience to consider the fluidity of gender and human desire. One way of looking at the play is to see it as challenging the idea that human sexuality is a clear-cut process: Olivia is attracted by the prettiness and verve of Viola; Orsino's feelings towards Viola are also complex. The ending of the play restores the main characters to the convention of heterosexual union, but consider Susie Campbell's observations:

 The end of the play resolves the issue on a superficial level. The fortuitous reappearance of Sebastian clears up the various confusions and ensures that the right partners end up together. But on a deeper level, nothing is resolved. Sebastian contributes to the equivocation around gender by assuring Olivia that she is marrying a 'maid and man' [...] Meanwhile, the Duke persists in calling Viola 'Boy' and 'Cesario' even after he has discovered that she is a woman. He seems quite happy to conflate the affection that he feels for his page with the romantic passion he sees as the proper feeling for a man to have for a woman.

 Activity 4

How far do you agree with the following views of love and desire in the play?

- The play celebrates love's power. It shows how love is blind and crosses boundaries of class and status. Love is beyond the control of the characters, who are driven by their desires, and often the very thing or person they think they need turns out to be the wrong choice. Love, like fate, is a force that operates outside of human control: it alone determines the nature of attraction and actual suitability of lovers.

- Love is shown to be powerful, but also troublesome. There is more heartache in the play than joy, and when the characters do find happiness, it's actually based on very little at all. Shakespeare shows how love is often little more than lust, and the formulaic words of love that are spoken in the play are meaningless. It's impossible to say that any character in the play finds true love.

- The play flirts with homosexual desire and allows the audience (and characters) to consider the boundaries of attraction, yet the play resolves to the socially sanctioned world of heterosexual pairings. Even then, there's enough doubt about these rapid pairings to suggest that conventional marriage will not necessarily bring satisfaction.

Deception

In comedy, deception can provoke humour. The deliberate misleading of others can cause laughter. In *Twelfth Night*, those forms of deception are acted out upon Malvolio and Sir Andrew, who both are offered misleading ideas about their chances with Olivia. You have already seen how there is debate around whether these actions are simply comic and/or perhaps cruel.

In the previous chapter you considered how the deception of the 'dark room' scene can be dramatized. You will have noticed how Malvolio is deceived by what appears to be the views of Sir Toby and others – that he is mad – but also by the disguise of Feste, another type of deception in the play. Read David Lewis's thoughts on the significance of deception in this scene:

 Feste's disguised voice (the visual disguise of gown and beard seems intended for the audience, as Malvolio cannot see him) deceives Malvolio into thinking that he is Sir Topas, but Malvolio stoutly refuses to accept any of Feste's deceptions or blatant lies [...] Feste, however, knows no restraint [...] Perhaps Fabian's curiously contradictory phrase 'sportful malice' (line 363) sums up our ambivalence towards the whole of this deception.

What does Viola's relationship with Orsino, both as Cesario and as herself, say about the nature of love?

The most significant deception is Viola's disguise. In choosing to become Cesario, she furthers the problems of the play. Her view that disguise is a 'wickedness' brings into question the light-hearted nature of disguise in comedy. Conventionally, disguise leads to jokes and merriment, before masks are cast aside and problems cleared up. In *Twelfth Night*, comic moments arise – the confusion of Sebastian and Viola leads to hilarious moments – but, although her disguise is thrown off, Viola remains 'Cesario' to Orsino, as if she is unable fully to escape the role she has created for herself.

Activity 5

Consider the idea that in the play disguise is a 'wickedness' rather than a light-hearted source of fun.

Another strand to the theme of deception is that of self-deception. This is a play that opens with a duke who convinces himself he has elaborate and genuine feelings for Olivia, yet the audience usually views him as misguided. In Illyria, it appears that a lack of self-knowledge besets the characters. The storylines of comedic texts usually show a movement from ignorance to knowledge, and in part this seems to apply to *Twelfth Night*. Journeys in comedy are often metaphorical: characters learn things about themselves and usually become more aware and therefore fulfilled by the final scenes.

Activity 6

a) Are all the characters in Illyria guilty of self-deception? Make a list of those who are and the nature of their misapprehensions.

Use a table like the one below to record your observations.

Character	Nature of their self-deception
Sir Andrew	He is under the impression that he is a suitable match for Olivia. He fails to see that his age, dimness and general buffoonery suggest otherwise. He also believes that Sir Toby is a good friend and doesn't realize that he is himself the butt of the joke. He is convinced of his talents with language and dancing, and feigns bravado. Whether he deceives himself in claiming that he was once loved isn't confirmed in the play.

b) Of the characters who appear to deceive themselves, which (if any) become more self-aware by the end of the text?

Madness and wisdom

Love in a way is a type of madness: it throws Olivia into an emotional state and provokes the uptight Malvolio to dress and behave outrageously. Madness is referred to several times in the play. Malvolio's exasperated remark in **'My masters are you mad?'** *(Act 2, Scene 3)* is directed at the revellers and is used in a broad sense to mean 'behaving inappropriately'. Feste deems Sir Toby a 'madman' in Act 1, Scene 5 in reference to his drunken state, and Olivia observes that Malvolio's ridiculous behaviour is **'very midsummer madness'** *(Act 3, Scene 4)*.

Malvolio is deemed mad – insane – in the plot against him, and incarcerated in a dark room as part of his 'treatment'. He insists **'do not think I am mad'** *(Act 4, Scene 2)* and protests **'I am as well in my wits as any man in Illyria'** *(Act 4, Scene 2)*. Malvolio isn't driven mad by the plotters, despite Feste's efforts, yet even he gives in to the madness of desire and fantasizes about his future with Olivia.

The play invites you to consider the ways in which the chaos of love and the topsy-turvy period of misrule infects the characters. It is possible to view many of the characters as displaying behaviour provoked by the madness of love or the more conscious madness of alcohol and festive mischief.

As noted earlier, Feste the fool appears to be the most aware character in the text. He is dubbed **'wise enough to play the fool'** by Viola *(Act 3, Scene 1)*, an observation that suggests that the insightful humour of Feste requires wisdom and judgement. As a truth-teller, Feste appears to possess a grasp of the failings and follies of humanity. There is a suggestion that the line between madness and sanity isn't always clearly defined: like words, the definition is unstable and, as the action shows, the madness of desire can cause rational people to act in ways that bring their judgment into question.

Malvolio and Feste show that the line between madness and sanity isn't always clear

---

Key quotation

But wise men, folly-fall'n, quite taint their wit
(Viola, Act 3, Scene 1)

 Activity 7

Consider the view that all the main characters are touched by madness in some form, be it festive unruliness or the 'plague' of love.

Cruelty and death

Comedies are conventionally light-hearted. They tend to suggest that disaster is possible, but never really likely. Tragedy is averted and the mood is one of uplift: comedy celebrates community and the things that make us happy. Villains, if they exist, are comic and get their comeuppance.

These conventions are echoed in *Twelfth Night*, yet there are unsettling aspects to the play, which tip the balance away from comedy. The play's downbeat opening scene feels heavy and introduces the idea of death and misery. Sir Toby's revelry can at times seem disorderly but not in a comic way. His disrespect for his niece's grief and manipulation of his friend jar a little. Feste's final song is one of pessimism and rain. Consider Kiernan Ryan's view:

 In *Twelfth Night* the spectre of death haunts the romantic protagonists' lives and loves from the start, and the scene begins to cloud toward the end from the moment the hoaxing of Malvolio turns into mental torment. It grows darker still when physical violence erupts into the play and the hitherto slap-happy sidekicks Sir Toby and Sir Andrew both stagger on with a 'bloody coxcomb' (V.i.173) inflicted by Sebastian, calling for 'Dick Surgeon' (V.i.195), who is too drunk himself to see to them.

Activity 8

Explore the following two views of the inclusion of cruelty and death in the play. Which, if any, do you agree with?

- The negative aspects shouldn't be taken too seriously. The violence where it occurs is comic and the punishment of Malvolio is playground humour. Rather than sympathize with Orsino's melancholy, we laugh – it's clear that we are being reminded that the posturing of some of the characters is laughable. Most comedies have some sort of darker edges and *Twelfth Night* is no different.

- The audience is never quite allowed to enjoy the comedy. There's always a sense the laughter is driven by someone else's misfortune. The play opens with misery and closes with it too. The 'happiness' of the main characters is a façade: those who will marry know little about each other, and too many characters on the fringes are treated cruelly.

A further way to consider the inclusion of cruelty and death in the play is to think about it in relation to genre. Perhaps Shakespeare invites us to consider the nature of comedy itself, reminding us that laughter often requires someone to be the butt of the joke, and that, in itself, is cruel. It may be that the play acts as both a celebration of comedy, but also a critique of it. In the years following, Shakespeare never really returned to the genre.

Later romances or late comedies such as *The Tempest* are less playful and more concerned with wider questions of life, ageing and forgiveness. Consider Kate Flint's view of the balance between entertainment and cruelty in *Twelfth Night* below:

> Whilst its plot is both preposterous and entertaining, its implications are far more serious. Even while the disguises, the role playing, the gulling and tricking are going on, there's an air of menace, of bullying, which is never far from the surface. Carnival, in other words, can be cruel; can tread on the edge of danger.

Key quotation

For the rain it raineth every day
(Feste, Act 5, Scene 1)

Activity 9

Consider the view that Shakespeare's play exposes the heartlessness at the heart of comedy.

Writing about themes

Upgrade

Writing about themes and ideas is effective when you make links across the text and explore how themes are developed and added to as the story progresses. Being aware of how an idea is introduced, and then how it is repeated and expanded in later parts of the narrative, is a useful way to bring together ideas about meanings and points about the playwright's method. Be alert to how one theme might be introduced mainly through one character's actions, but is then mirrored through another character.

Other structural ideas such as contrast are useful starting points for illuminating work on themes. For instance, you might compare the ways in which the love Viola has for Orsino contrasts with that of Sir Toby and Maria. You should also consider the extent to which themes such as appearance and reality are explored in numerous contexts. Linking themes to backdrops such as gender, power and social matters are valuable ways to tie in points about meaning and context.

Performance

Decisions made by a director and actors strongly influence the way a character or scene is received by the audience. If you read a novel, the action takes place in your head. However, a drama script takes place on stage, and there is a group of people – the director and actors – who create an interpretation of the play, one which may or may not coincide with the version you have in your head.

Stage directions in *Twelfth Night* are minimal so there is plenty of scope for how scenes may be performed and how lines may be delivered. As you study the play, be alert to the ways in which performance context can affect the way the play is interpreted. As ever, there is no one 'correct' reading of the play.

Performance history

Being able to cite details of various performances over the centuries is of little use in itself, but noticing the general patterns or fashions for ways of staging the play and the concepts behind them can be illuminating. In *Make a Good Show On't: Twelfth Night in Performance*, the point is made that in the past 50 years, there have been two broad approaches to setting the play: the festive versions (ones with a seasonal aspect) and the 'Illyrian' versions (ones that have fantastical qualities). Both offer the audience interesting staging choices.

Festive or seasonal interpretations of the play have included Peter Hall's 1958 version, John Barton's 1969 take on the play and Terry Hands's 1979 'reading of the comedy as a life-renewing seasonal passage from snow-laden and frosty-branched midwinter to daffodilly spring' (dramaonlinelibrary.com). In Hands's version, the idea seems to suggest that love unfreezes winter's discontent and moves characters into a new realm. A further production in this festive mode was offered by Kenneth Branagh in 1987:

 [Branagh's production was] staged at the winter solstice, in keeping with its primarily subdued and at times funereal atmosphere: 'He has taken the title literally and his Edwardian Illyria is locked in the grip of an icy winter,' observed Charles Spencer (*Daily Telegraph*). Bunnie Christy's main set was a snow-covered cemetery littered with 'balustrades, broken masonry, scattered statuary, ivy-twined gates, bare trees' (Martin Hoyle, *Financial Times*). Branagh also made the increasingly popular choice of a Victorian-to-Edwardian Christmas setting, with decorated tree and all.

'Illyrian' versions of the play, which offer a more exotic interpretation, have included Hugh Hunt's 1950 production in an Italian (rather than English) setting and Michael Kahn's 1989 production set on an eastern island occupied by the British. These versions often hint at a **postcolonial** reading of the play, which looks at the tensions and hierarchies present in countries colonized by Western powers in earlier centuries.

Sir Andrew, Fabian and Sir Toby shiver behind the Christmas tree in Branagh's production.

Stephen Beresford's 2004 production envisioned Illyria as Indian, in which:

 The transposition of Illyrian events to modern-day India was posited on a powerful analogy between the early modern class hierarchy and the Indian caste system, above all in the relationship between householders and their servants. [...] The production opened spectacularly with a monsoon lashing down on shuttered houses in Jonathan Fensom's set, which was tilted at an angle so as to suggest a world emotionally out of joint.

postcolonial an approach to interpreting a text which looks at issues of power and control in those cultures affected by colonization; also, a text type – one set in countries that experienced colonization and its aftermath

 Activity 1

Of the two dominant versions of the play, which do you think offers the more appealing interpretation of the text? For you, is *Twelfth Night* a seasonal English play, or an exotic and fantastical one?

 Activity 2

Using websites such as dramaonlinelibrary.com and theatrehistory.com as starting points, explore the production history of the play. Are there any patterns in the way the play was produced in earlier centuries? *Twelfth Night* has always been popular as a theatrical event. Which qualities lend themselves to performance?

Metatheatricality

Twelfth Night has a **metatheatrical** quality. It has:

- role-playing (Feste as Sir Topas, Viola as Cesario)
- lines that draw attention to performance (Viola's **'I am not that I play'**, *Act 1, Scene 5*)
- frequent references to exits and entrances – there are many lines in which doors and gates are mentioned.

There is a sense in which the audience are reminded of the play's artifice – that they are watching a play that is fantastical in nature. Part of this is an echo of the comedy genre, which frequently involves getting the audience to laugh along and engage in the playful aspect of the performance (something tragedy never does).

Part of the joke for the original audiences (and also those who see modern all-male cast versions) is that Viola was played by a male dressed as a female, who then disguises herself as a male. Fabian's line in Act 3, Scene 4 – **'If this were played upon a stage now, I could condemn it as an improbable fiction'** – has a heavily ironic application for the rest of the play. It does seem that the play invites the audience to always be aware that this is a performance.

> **metatheatrical** where a play contains lines or events that draw attention to its own play-like qualities

Activity 3

Explore the idea that because the audience is frequently reminded of the artifice of the play, then nothing is really taken too seriously. Even when Malvolio is 'tortured', we are made aware of the performance aspects (Feste's role-playing and disguise) so it is always viewed as playful, rather than horrific.

Performance as a reading

Period setting, costume, gesture, body language and delivery all contribute to performance and, in deciding such things, a reading of a text is produced. One way to explore the importance of performance context is to consider what sort of decisions you might make.

The lines from **'A sister! You are she'** to *'And we'll strive to please you every day'* (*Act 5, Scene 1*) form the final part of the play, which includes Malvolio's exit, Orsino's closing speech and Feste's final song. In performance, many decisions have to be made which contribute to the overall effect. For instance, look at the 8 decisions to be made opposite, on page 87.

- What is the overriding emotion portrayed by Malvolio when he enters the stage at the start of this section? Is he furious or a quaking, broken man? Would you want the audience still to view him as pompous when he refers to the **'lighter people'** or should they feel sympathy?

- Is Olivia's reaction to Malvolio consistent in this scene? How is her line **'Have I, Malvolio? No!'** delivered? Is it mock exasperation? Does she titter as she looks at the steward? At which point, if at all, does her attitude change? Olivia has been tricked too. Is she taken aback by these revelations?

- How do the other onstage characters behave as Malvolio is ranting (if indeed this is what he is doing)? Are they laughing behind their hands? Is there any sense in which they feel ashamed?

- How is Fabian's justification – **'How with a sportful [...] both sides pass'd'** – received by Olivia? Does she nod acceptingly or glare at him disapprovingly? In her next two lines to Malvolio, how much feeling towards his plight is conveyed in her voice? Is there any hint that she is stifling a laugh or is she genuinely sympathetic?

- How much anger is conveyed in Malvolio's parting line? Is this a serious threat accompanied by silence as he leaves? Does he storm off? Or does he leave the stage with the derisory laughter of the other characters ringing in his ears? If the characters do laugh, should the audience share this laughter, or is there a jarring note?

- How should Orsino be portrayed? Is he a commanding force who stage-manages the lines from **'Pursue him...'** to **'... fancy's queen'**? Or is there an oddity about his wish to refer to his intended wife as 'Cesario'? Does he appear foppish? How is the exit of the characters shown? Is it celebratory? Do they leave arm-in-arm?

- Viola is on stage in this part of Act 5, Scene 1, but she is silent. What instruction should be given to the actor playing this part? How should she behave towards Orsino? Deferential? Is she now his property? How should she act when he tells her that he will refer to her as Cesario?

- How should Feste deliver his song? Is it sardonic or should it be bitingly sarcastic? Should the audience be nodding ruefully as Feste recounts the disappointment of marriage? Some performances end with a dance by the whole cast. Is this appropriate? Or is this a melancholy ending?

Activity 4

Re-read the passage in Act 5, Scene 1 from **'A sister! You are she'** to **'And we'll strive to please you every day'**. Then consider the points above. What choices would you make? What overall effect do you feel needs to be achieved in this extract?

Activity 5

Think further about the final section of the play. Consider these descriptions of ways of performing the scene. Which, if any, coincides with your view of this extract?

Performance A

This is a moment of high drama. Malvolio storms on stage and speaks abruptly to his boss and social superior. Olivia, although taken aback, is sympathetic to his plight: their professional relationship is one of trust and, as Malvolio speaks, the other characters are still, anticipating problems. Olivia, however, is calm and supports him. She is less tolerant of Fabian, glowering at him as he shuffles nervously, attempting to justify the trick. Feste's gloating increases the tension and Malvolio storms off to silence. Orsino's final speech is an anticlimax, however. His words are hollow and out of touch with what has gone before. Feste's song is delivered in a monotone and the play ends on a sour note.

Performance B

The final part of Act 5, Scene 1 is a largely good-humoured affair with Malvolio the butt of the joke. As he speaks, the humour lies in his comic frustration. Even Olivia has to control her laughter as the trick becomes obvious to her. While trying to keep a straight face, she placates him. As he storms off like a petulant teenager, there is a pause, after which all the onstage characters burst into laughter. Streamers and party poppers explode. Orsino knowingly winks at Viola as he declares her 'Cesario': he clearly anticipates a playful evening ahead. Feste's song is performed with a conscious irony: he is satirizing his own misanthropic persona. The performance ends with a rousing song and dance in which the whole cast – even Malvolio – appear to have stepped out of their roles. The audience leave the theatre happy. It's comedy: everyone is okay.

Activity 6

Re-read the lines from 'Here comes the Countess...' to 'thou hast too much fear' (Act 5, Scene 1) and think about the different ways they might be performed. Write out two differing versions, using the models above for Performance A and Performance B as templates.

Concepts underpinning performance

Most directors begin with an overall concept of the play and use this to inform key decisions about staging, costume and movement. Some productions are set in what might be considered a traditional way, adopting versions of 17th-century costume and using staging that suggests the fantastical world of Illyria. Other directors select modern dress and place the text in a more modern landscape, which can help an audience to see the play through fresh eyes, or perhaps make the point that the play's ideas are universal to any time.

Activity 7

Explore ways in which you might stage the 'dark room' scene in Act 4, Scene 2. This scene is crucial in terms of the general concept of the play. Should the audience see Malvolio's treatment as torture or fun? Consider:

- Where would Malvolio be positioned? Is he below stage in a dungeon and, if so, what can the audience see of him?

- How should Sir Toby and Maria act during Feste's performance as Sir Topas?

- How could lighting be used to aid the overall effect?

Read the extracts on page 90 from '"Why, we shall make him mad indeed": directing the dark room scene', an essay in which Bill Alexander discusses the process of how he and the cast decided to perform Act 4, Scene 2 in his 1987 RSC version of the play. In his production, Alexander decided to have Malvolio on stage.

Malvolio was imprisoned in a cage in the Nottingham Playhouse production of 1995

[We] came up with the idea of his being chained to a post, just as bears used to be in bear-baiting. It fitted in with the suggestion we wanted to give of his being the victim of a cruel sport, of being tortured like an animal.

 [Once] we had decided on the bear-post, one of the two actors playing Malvolio and Feste – I don't remember which – suddenly said, why didn't we actually set the scene in the dark room itself? We could let the audience see Feste descending a ladder, to make it quite clear that he was going down to join Malvolio in his prison cell.

That meant, of course, that we had to re-think what to do with Sir Toby and Maria, who are normally on stage for the first half of the scene. Originally, we had planned to have Sir Toby dancing around behind Feste, taking great delight in what was going on, with Maria egging him on. But now, instead of that, we decided to place the two of them up at the back of the stage, looking down from a tiny window. We would have them embracing each other, kissing each other – clearly enjoying listening to Malvolio's distress and even seeming to get a perverse kick out of it.

Then suddenly someone remembered the *Black Comedy* idea. *Black Comedy* is a play by Peter Schaffer that takes place in darkness. But instead of being in darkness, the stage is in fact brightly lit […] Instead of dimming the whole stage, we would flood a certain area of it with dazzlingly bright light to delineate the dark room. Both Feste and Malvolio would have their eyes open. But it would be clear to the audience from the very first moment – by the way they moved around the stage – that neither of them would be able to see a thing.

 The use of light in this way would heighten the farce of the scene. But it would also heighten its cruelty. Not a single wince or grimace would go unnoticed. Like so much of the play, there is a blend in this scene between humour and horror.

 Activity 8

What do you think Bill Alexander was trying to achieve in his version of the play? What overall concept underpins the decisions and how closely does it match your interpretation of the play?

Performing character

Directors and actors make decisions about the specifics of character. Choices about body language, delivery of key lines and costume all affect how a character comes across. Watching as many versions of the play as possible will alert you to the variety of ways in which character can be played. For now, consider these three accounts of character performance as described in Paul Edmondson's *The Shakespeare Handbooks: Twelfth Night*.

> Malvolio was possessed of all the wild and dangerous qualities which Nicol Williamson was known for bringing onto the stage [...] his tight-lipped authority was expressed with a slightly hesitant and softly spoken voice which in the main only used his bottom lip. It was a grotesque performance, with something of the simmering Scottish pastor about it, replete with a proud crane-like walk.

> John Price's Orsino was first discovered lounging on cushions [...] Orsino, bare chested, medallioned, and loosely clothed was clearly entranced [...] Viola was sitting in a curled position between Orsino's legs, close enough for her left leg to be in complete contact with his. He took hold of her head and turned it intimately towards him.

> Olivia entered and felt her own breasts in a private moment of sexual fantasy (III. iv.1–4). At her entrance in Act IV, Scene i she brandished a bondage-style whip. She had finally come to take complete control of Cesario (now Sebastian) and cracked the whip with authority, catching the back of Sir Andrew's ankles as he hurried off stage. In contrast, Viola seemed curiously sexless.

Activity 9

Viola can be played in a variety of ways. Select some key scenes involving Viola – perhaps Act 1, Scene 5 or Act 3, Scene 1 – and experiment with how clothing, action, delivery of lines and body language might bring out different interpretations of her character. Is she the feisty go-getter, or is she suffering for love and waiting hopefully for time to untie the knot of problems?

Performing gender and sexuality

The original performances of the play would have featured an all-male cast, throwing up interesting issues around sexuality. The hilarious 2012 Globe production of the play featured an all-male cast. Try to watch the filmed version of this, noting how the actors' gender gives rise to humour.

As you have seen in the previous descriptions of the performance of Orsino and Olivia, some versions of the play make much of gender and issues around sexuality. Peter Gill's 1974 RSC version used the visual image of Narcissus to suggest self-love and issues of bisexuality. Likewise, Trevor Nunn's 1996 film version, although it played around with the original text, offered some interesting ideas about desire:

> In the movie's most sensual moment, the disguised Viola gives Orsino a sponge bath, practically drooling over his naked body as he confides his lovesick fantasies […] In calmly presenting the homoerotic elements of these tangled connections, the movie suggests that an essential sexual ambiguity exists in all of us once the defining plumage of one sex has been exchanged for that of the other. Having turned herself into a boy, Viola, whom Ms. Stubbs plays with a chipper wide-eyed smirk, gamely learns how to play billiards, smoke cigars and ride horses.

The 2017 National Theatre production offered a further striking take on sexuality, choosing to swap the gender of Malvolio:

> As Malvolio – here Malvolia – Tamsin Greig joins the list of women playing major Shakespearean roles. It's a masterstroke of casting. She doesn't just steal her scenes she starts up her own black market. Hers is a performance of great comic skill. As Olivia's uptight steward, she has the manner of an Agatha Christie school mistress with her sensible culottes and ruler-straight hair. She walks with odd little rabbit-like steps. She stares longingly at Olivia when she sleeps. She is a figure of fun. She's also a lesbian, and this results in some moments that skirt uneasily close to stereotype, but Greig rises above this, engaging with the audience and conveying the full extent of the hurt and humiliation that her character is subjected to.

Tamsin Greig played Malvolio in the 2017 National Theatre production.

Activity 10

The two productions referred to in these reviews raise a lot of gender issues. To what extent do you think these production choices illuminate the play, or are they a little superficial and add little to the meaning of the text?

Film versions of the play

As you have just seen, film versions offer a different opportunity to play with the text, often altering dialogue or having the luxury to switch quickly between the sort of lavish sets that can't be reproduced on stage. Kenneth Branagh's 1988 film (a festive *Twelfth Night*) offered a 'nasty' Feste, while Trevor Nunn's 1996 version used location to reinforce meaning. Paul Edmondson in *The Shakespeare Handbooks: Twelfth Night* describes Nunn's decisions thus:

 … a pervasive autumnal tone throughout: muted colours, unapologetically darkened interiors, apples being harvested in the orchard. There is a distinct and ever-present melancholy ready to break through into the comedy. Filmed partly on location on the Cornish coast, it continually reminds the viewer of the sweeping presence and metaphorical power of the ocean; of time passing, a reminder of the futility of human endeavor, and mortality.

Activity 11

Explore the differences between Trevor Nunn's 1996 film and the 2012 filmed Globe stage version of the play. Compare the choices that the film directors and stage directors make in relation to the text. What significant differences are there?

Writing about performance

In your writing, you will need to use performance context carefully. There is no advantage in listing features of various productions you may have seen unless they are directly relevant to the question that faces you. Writing about performance works best when linked to the overarching concepts and ideas in the play.

If you are exploring an extract from *Twelfth Night* closely, you may well choose to focus on a specific key line from the text and write about various ways the performance of that line might give rise to different readings of character.

Be careful not to confuse the study of literature with theatre studies – the primary focus is the text and its meanings. Dramatic method and performance aspects should only support the points you make about the literary aspects of the play.

Twelfth Night is a play that has generated many critical responses. The changing contexts in which the play is performed and received have ensured that the play has a long critical history. Literary criticism can illuminate your understanding of the play and help you view its content from different angles. Careful reading and critical assessment of such views is very important.

> ### Activity 1
>
> As a starting point for your study of critical views, explore early responses to *Twelfth Night*, such as John Manningham's account of the play. He was a lawyer and diarist writing during the Elizabethan and Jacobean periods.

Reading approaches

Critical opinions about texts are personal responses, but they are never free from the cultural baggage and prejudices of the person who writes them. Although it is tempting to read critical opinion as simply a person's individual response, they embody the values of the person and the society in which the response is written. The approach critics adopt says a lot about what they think is the 'correct' or most illuminating way to read literature.

Essentialist criticism, an older approach, which analysed characters as if they were 'real', has largely been overtaken by approaches that see literature as **representational criticism**. This means judging characters and texts as representations of society. Therefore the task of the reader/critic is to look at the representation offered in the text and to explore the ideology (view of the world) it proposes.

> **essentialist criticism** looking for the essence of a character itself, as if the character had a 'real' existence
>
> **representational criticism** seeing characters and situations as constructs – versions of 'real' characters and events; representational readings place emphasis on how they have been shown by the writer and what they reveal about the values of society and the writer

Two central approaches or schools of thought on how literature can be read are Marxist criticism and gender criticism.

Marxist criticism

This takes its cue from the political beliefs originating in the views of Karl Marx, an economist and philosopher. Adopting a Marxist approach to reading literature means exploring the representation of power, class and status in the world of the text. Marx's view was that economic situations determine everything in the real world. This means that analysing the interaction of social and economic factors in the text, and also the conditions in which the text was produced, is central to any reading.

Adopting a Marxist approach to reading literature also requires acknowledging that human beings are less free than they might think, and that our idea of 'the way the world works' is an illusion. The prevailing ideology is designed by those in power to keep them in power. The powerless, by contrast, see this ideology as 'common sense' and 'normal' rather than anything that could be challenged. Consequently, Marxist critics look closely at issues of conflict, ideology and class struggle in the world of the text.

Activity 2

Consider the role of power and status in the play. You could explore:

- The power structures in Orsino's palace. How does the dialogue reflect the way power operates?

- The position of Sir Toby in his niece's house. As a character with the social status of a knight, is he afforded special treatment? Do you see this play as a criticism of privilege and status?

Gender criticism

This looks at the ways literature represents masculinity and femininity. Readers exploring texts from this angle take the view that literature can promote negative images of gender, helping to support stereotypes rather than challenge them. Females, for example, might be portrayed in narrow roles as virginal or whorish, helpless or shrewish. Exploring the depiction of both genders can reveal a lot about the way society and the writer view men and women.

There is an assumption that the general reader is male, and that the sorts of texts promoted by educational institutions are mainly the work of dead, white males. Feminist critics explore and expose the view that to be male and heterosexual is 'normal' and to be female or gay is to be 'different'.

Activity 3

Consider the role of gender in the play. You could explore:

- What masculinity means in the play. How much of it is bound up with toughness and power? Are men ever 'weak' in the text? If so, what happens to them?

- Whether females in the play are always victims. Are they always represented as powerless unless they are disguised or bequeathed power by the deaths of male relatives?

- Whether Olivia might be read positively as a woman who asserts herself and stands up to the power of Orsino.

Activity 4

There are many other critical theories and approaches that could inform your study of *Twelfth Night*. Some theoretical approaches are relatively new and still evolving. Some approaches are complex and demand careful study. Research the following areas and their potential usefulness to your reading of the play:

- postcolonialism

- narrative and narratology

- psychoanalytical

- eco-criticism

- postmodernism.

Tips for assessment

If you want to include a quotation from a critical piece in your own essay, make sure it supports the point you are trying to make, and use it to strengthen your argument, rather than to make the point for you. Your arguments must be your own.

Beginning to apply critical views

As you begin to explore published critical views, take time to understand the arguments being proposed, the approach being taken and, crucially, whether you agree with what is being said or not.

Activity 5

Read Text A, taking careful note of the main points of the argument, which have been highlighted.

TEXT A

 Malvolio does not deserve the destructively relentless mockery which he receives. If he seems a kill-joy, it's chiefly because it's his job to be not only an errand-boy and general manager but also the household policeman – though a powerless and unarmed policeman. If he displays some egoistic vanity in imagining himself to be loved by Olivia, that seems harmless enough; Sir Andrew has similar delusions. Any critic who suggests that sympathy for Malvolio is anachronistic, a modern sentimentality alien to the tougher Elizabethan sensibility, is refuted by the text, for […] it is not Malvolio alone but also the perceptive Olivia who regards his humiliation as excessive.

Activity 6

Explore the ideas highlighted in Text A. Consider:

- is the reading that Malvolio doesn't deserve mockery a convincing argument?
- does Olivia take Malvolio's side entirely?

Activity 7

Use Text B below to practise your critical reading skills. Read the interpretation and then:

- identify the key point being made about Orsino's character
- find references and events in the play to support or challenge the reading proposed
- write a response, pulling your points and evidence together, which considers how convincing you think this opinion of Orsino is.

TEXT B

 When Orsino appears again in the final act, his actions render his character revelation complete. Both the rapidity with which he can turn angrily on Olivia and the poised alacrity with which he can accept Cesario (now Viola) as his heart's substitute reveal how deeply indeed has been his commitment to the stakes of love! When the countess first enters in Act V, Orsino speaks metaphorically of heaven walking on earth. But, his suit again rejected as 'fat and fulsome,' he suddenly alters his metaphor to 'perverseness,' 'uncivil lady,' and, instead of heaven and its shrines, speaks of her 'ingrate and inauspicious altars'.

Interpreting character

In the previous activities and throughout this book, you have seen how it is possible to respond to characters in a variety of ways. In Text C below, Michael Gearin-Tosh makes several judgments about Olivia and Feste.

Activity 8

Read Text C and consider:

- Is this an accurate view of the way Olivia acts in the final scene, and what is being implied about her attitude to the plot against Malvolio? Is there any reason why Olivia might be shown to act in this way?

- Do you agree that Feste's motives are to be frowned upon? Where do your sympathies lie?

TEXT C

 Events move quickly in the final seconds of *Twelfth Night* and Shakespeare allows no room for comment. But it is notable that Olivia does not console Feste for his pain as she had done Malvolio. Her response is a simple but eloquent cry: 'He hath been most notoriously abused' (V.1.376).

We accept Olivia as the voice of real discernment in the earlier quarrel between Feste and Malvolio and we should do so here. She does not attempt to strike a balance between the injuries of Feste and Malvolio, as Fabian had done with those of Malvolio and Toby. Making a fair judgement diverts us from whether we should be judging at all, and throws a cloak of respectability over an activity which is generally too detached to be loving. Olivia sees that whatever the merits of Feste's case, his manner undermines them. She acted as a peacemaker, he renews ill feeling. And what are his motives? Feste humiliates Malvolio by reminding him of his social ambitions in front of Olivia, Sebastian and Orsino, where it could not be more embarrassing.

Interpreting comedy

In these next two pieces of criticism, the writers explore the nature of the comedy and how it can be viewed. Thinking about the play against the backdrop of comedy is something you have been doing throughout this book, and it is an approach that allows you to stand back from the play as a single entity and see how it sits against the body of a genre.

Activity 9

Read Texts D and E carefully and consider whether:

- the play always mixes pleasure and pain
- the play offers you 'sobering lessons' about life
- the ending of the play shows the characters in a state of stasis
- the joyful parts of the play give you a brief respite from the adversity of real life.

TEXT D

To highlight the more disturbing aspects of the play is, I believe, to return to the Renaissance spirit of carnival: to its knife-edge between the violent and the ridiculous, where the human body itself becomes a figure for spectacle […] The fact that not only is there no feast without cruelty, but that the world of carnival, mingling pleasure with pain, merely exaggerates tendencies to be found in real life rather than providing an escape from them, is the sobering lesson which *Twelfth Night* teaches us.

Feste could be interpreted as the only truly free character in the play.

TEXT E

For the romantic protagonists of this comedy there will be no voyage back from the virtual reality in which Shakespeare has marooned them. The completeness of their enclosure in the illusory universe of Illyria is underscored by Viola's continuous disguise, from which she's fated never to emerge to embrace her brother and claim her husband on stage. Only when 'golden time convents' (V.i.378) shall she and Orsino 'have share in this most happy wreck' (V.i.264) and the 'solemn combination' of both couples' 'dear souls' (V.i.379–80) be made. There Shakespeare leaves them, in a perpetual state of elated anticipation, which will never be satisfied, but which can never be disappointed. As for us, we have no choice but to return with Feste to the world outside the theatre, a world whipped by the wind and lashed by the rain, where adversity and dismay rather than delight seem to be the rule, but where, as *Twelfth Night* has been at pains to teach us, nothing that is so, is so, and glimpses of golden times abound.

Interpreting narrative

Rather than focus upon character or theme, some criticism looks at the way in which texts are structured and the effects that are generated. Texts F–I look at the playwright's choices of subtitle, plot and subplot, entrances and dialogue.

Activity 10

The play's subtitle, *What You Will*, can be read in several ways. Read Text F and consider whether:

- the subtitle is an invitation to the audience to take from the play what they wish

- it's Shakespeare saying to the audience 'here you go – the sort of funny play you like' while undercutting that at the same time with the inclusion of death and cruelty

- the double meaning of 'will' is a nod to the lust and desire in the text.

TEXT F

 Although the main meaning of the word 'will' in the play's title is 'wish' or 'want', in Elizabethan usage it could also signify irrational desire, unbridled passion, as Shakespeare's persistent puns on the word in his sonnets to the Dark Lady testify. This sense lurks in *'or What You Will'* too, adumbrating the play's concern with characters seized by a blind infatuation or consuming emotion. In this respect, the alternative title reinforces the carnivalesque connotations of *'Twelfth Night'*: it primes us to expect violations of sexual propriety.

Activity 11

Read Text G. What do you think is meant by the view that the trick on Malvolio is a prelude to later character revelations?

TEXT G

 The close integration of the subplot reveals further the careful construction of the plot of *Twelfth Night*. Malvolio's puritanical posture as the zealous moralist and the flagrant exposure of his hypocrisy by Feste and Maria reinforce both the theme of character revelation and the tone of tolerant mockery [...] Thematically, Malvolio is a third suitor for Olivia in Acts II and III, his presumptuous wooing occurring as a corollary to Olivia's ridiculous pursuit of Viola-Cesario. Structurally, Shakespeare utilizes the gulling and exposure of Malvolio (II, iv; III; iv) as a prelude to the major character revelations in Act IV.

In Text H, the writer proposes that Sebastian's arrival and onstage presence is:

- the most dramatic moment of the play
- a symbol of the play's confusions.

Do you agree with these views?

TEXT H

The entrance of Sebastian is 'what we will'. It is the most dramatic moment of the play. The confrontation of Sebastian and Cesario-Viola, those identical images, concludes the formal plot and provides the means for the discarding of all the lovers' masks. The moment must be savored and fully realized. As Viola and Sebastian chant their traditional formulas of proof, both the audience and the other characters on the stage undistractedly view the physical image of duality which has made the confusion and the play.

The view in Text I suggests that the dialogue in scenes set in Olivia's house is largely liberal and slightly chaotic.

- Does the text bear out this view?
- What is the nature of the dialogue in scenes set in Orsino's palace?

TEXT I

Throughout the play a contrast is maintained between the taut, restless, elegant court, where people speak a nervous verse, and the free-wheeling household of Olivia, where, except for the intense moments in Olivia's amorous interviews with Cesario, people live in an easy-going prose. [...] The household is more than any one person in it. People keep interrupting each other, changing their minds, letting their talk run out into foolishness – and through it all Shakespeare expresses the day-by-day going on of a shared life.

Interpreting endings

Endings of any texts are important. They are the points where stories close and meanings are most likely to be found. As you have already seen, the ending of *Twelfth Night* seems superficially comedic, but there are more troubling aspects. Texts J and K offer ways of thinking about the ending.

Activity 14

How much of the final scene is about distress? Read Text J and consider whether the ending of the play is actually happy in any sense.

TEXT J

For a play which, at one level, ends like a conventional comedy, with the happy pairing off of lovers, the whole of the last scene, in fact, is surprisingly permeated by violence and death. Antonio, the sea-captain who rescued Sebastian, has been arrested and is in danger of his life. The dreadful wrangle between Orsino, Viola and Olivia is broken into by Sir Toby with a 'bloody coxcomb'; his head has been damaged, indeed, by Sebastian, who even though he enters justifying his action – an entry which allows the play to move towards its resolution – hardly, therefore, appears as a peaceful saviour. Moreover, his own language is full of physical distress.

Activity 15

Text K links the meaning of the play to the work of another more modern playwright. Read Text K and then:

a) Read plot summaries of some of the plays of Samuel Beckett.

b) Consider whether the characters really are shown to be shallow and cruel.

c) Consider whether *Twelfth Night* is close to the concerns of some modern playwrights, whose work shows the emptiness of life.

TEXT K

Twelfth Night as a whole seems to be a play about a decadent society where people's feelings are not to be trusted […] it is a play, I suggest, that presents an audience with a bleak picture of the human condition. The men and women portrayed within it are repeatedly revealed as shallow, foolish, and capable of extreme cruelty. Even the names of some of the characters – Belch, Aguecheek, Feste – seem to conjure the smell of decay […] Sir Toby Belch is only too keen to exploit the trusting friendship of the simple Sir Andrew, and quick to resort to violence when encountering Sebastian. The world he inhabits seems closer to the empty and ultimately meaningless landscape of Samuel Beckett's plays than it does to the sunlit uplands of Shakespeare's other comedies.

Developing your own readings

Critical views are useful in provoking thought and inviting you to look at the play from different angles. They should be exercised with caution and engaged with, rather than taken as 'correct' viewpoints. The most important view of the play's elements is your own. Any response you give to the play will be ultimately your own views, although it may well be informed by those of other readers and published critical opinions.

Part of the process of generating your own opinion of the play may be helped by applying the different reading approaches mentioned at the start of this chapter. Although there are different types of gender and Marxist criticism, considering how these sorts of approaches might make you see the play in different ways can be a useful starting point.

Activity 16

Re-read Act 2, Scene 4. Consider how different reading approaches might help you generate views of this part of the play.

a) Explore the representations of gender in this extract. What significant aspects of masculinity and femininity are shown? What is the balance of power between male and female? Is it possible to say that familiar stereotypes of men and women are employed?

b) Look closely at the nature of power and status. What is shown about the way social structures operate here? Although she occupies a lesser social status in the world of the text, do Viola's actions and words reflect this?

c) Using your observations, write a close analysis of Act 2, Scene 4 in terms of the issues relating to gender and power. Adopt a critical approach that you think best suits the way you wish to interpret the play. Use Texts A–K in this chapter as models of the way in which you might write your response.

Writing about critical views

When you read criticism in conjunction with *Twelfth Night*, you are effectively juggling two texts. Critical views are essentially 'writing about writing' and are, in the end, just views. Rather than taking a critical view at face value, it is important that you first of all understand what is being said and, secondly, that you evaluate it. Read criticism *critically*. You should test views out and see if you agree with them – or not. Never just refer to a view. Look at the strengths and weaknesses of the reading.

Exam skills

Effective responses to literature are grounded in an understanding of the text. If you are confident about the plot, structure, characters, settings, themes and genre elements of *Twelfth Night*, you will be able to select wisely the 'right' material to focus upon in your writing.

Whether you set your own questions or respond to tasks given to you, writing about *Twelfth Night* at A/AS level requires you to work on your phrasing skills; take account of dramatic method, context and genre; and, most importantly, focus closely on the question you are presented with. Invariably, A/AS level tasks will ask more specific questions, sometimes offering debates to respond to or an extract to comment on. The quality of your ideas, the strength of your argument, and your own personal voice will be central to any piece of writing you construct. Refining your thinking and discussion skills is essential.

Focusing on the task

Questions, or tasks as they are often termed, require an answer. The wording of a task is carefully crafted to stimulate your thoughts and point you in certain directions. Ignoring the task and simply writing 'everything I know about the play' will result in a poor essay. Similarly, taking a question and 'warping' it so you can write about what you know best (rather than the actual question you've been given) will also have a disastrous outcome. Focusing on the task in hand and looking at the key words in the question is the starting point of an effective answer.

Activity 1

Look carefully at the following task. What are the key words? What precisely is the task inviting you to do?

> How far do you agree that Shakespeare presents misrule as a light-hearted and hilarious aspect of *Twelfth Night*?

The first thing you might have noticed is the invitation to offer an opinion. This is carried in the first five words of this task: 'How far do you agree…'. The use of the second person pronoun should alert you to the fact that this type of task is asking for *your* opinion. It is therefore important that your response does provide *your* opinion, and you must come to a conclusion.

The first five words also tell you that there is some sort of debate being set up. There are two strands to the debate: first that misrule is 'light-hearted' and second that it is 'hilarious'. It is possible to take issue with or support one or both of these interpretations. Any effective essay will need to work very closely with the key terms and build an argument around them.

You will also have recognized that the term 'misrule' is a term related to a comedic concept – that of rebelliousness and a deliberate flouting of the rules – so the parts of the text you choose to write about must be related to that.

The term 'light-hearted' introduces both a generic and a cultural concept – that of amusement. In comedic literature, 'light-hearted' signifies something that is playful and inconsequential. You should also bring in your own cultural understanding of what 'light-hearted' means. This will differ between readers – what one person defines as 'light-hearted' might mean something different to another reader: comedy, as ever, asks you to decide where the limits of humour lie.

The term 'hilarious' is also a relative concept. You have seen how some of the ways you might interpret the rebellious behaviour of the characters is open to interpretation, and this task is asking how *you* see it. Is it only 'light-hearted'? Is it accurately described as 'hilarious'? Or is there something more troubling about the nature of misrule in the play?

Another aspect of the task is carried in the words 'Shakespeare presents'. Here you are being reminded that there is a playwright who carefully shapes and arranges the material. You are being asked to look at how the playwright structures the text: what he has the characters doing in relation to unruly behaviour, the exits and entrances, the character arc, the words used, and so on. Remember that writing about method doesn't mean *writing anything* about method: it must be relevant to the task, so any points you make about method must serve the key terms 'misrule', 'light-hearted' and 'hilarious'.

So in summary the task requires you to debate the ideas that misrule is light-hearted and hilarious, and think about the playwright's methods as you do so. Implicit in all of this are the assumptions that you will write clearly and fluently, and use evidence – quotations or references – to support your points.

Some reminders

Writing effective essays shouldn't be reduced to a checklist. Formulaic responses run the risk of being straitjacketed, rather than interesting and creative. It is possible, however, to use the following prompts to judge the quality of your own work:

- How closely do I focus on the key terms in the task?
- How well do I get involved in the debate?
- What is the quality of my argument? How convincing is it?
- Is my essay well structured and fluently written?
- Do I write relevantly about the playwright's methods?

Activity 2

Using the list of prompts on the previous page, read the following sample student responses and judge the quality of each answer. They are both partial answers to the following task:

> How far do you agree that Shakespeare presents misrule as a light-hearted and hilarious aspect of *Twelfth Night*?

Sample answer 1

There are plenty of examples of humour in Twelfth Night. One of them is when Viola is dressed as a page but Orsino doesn't realize. In that scene, Viola has decided to work for Orsino, even though she is struggling to handle the possible death of her brother, so although the death aspect of the story isn't funny, when she is dressed as a boy it looks funny for the audience. This is because the actress wears male clothing and it is quite obvious to the audience that Viola is female, but Orsino doesn't get it – he foolishly thinks Viola is male. Orsino calls her 'lad' and says she has a 'maiden's organ', which all sounds funny because the two ideas of being male and female are contrasts. He also says she has 'Diana's lip', another funny phrase.

Sample answer 2

Twelfth Night invites the audience to consider the rebellious hilarity of misrule, but also its shortcomings. Temporarily at least, the playful disrespect of authority causes laughter: Sir Toby's carefree dismissal of Malvolio's puritanical approach to life can, in the theatre, prove hilarious. Prior to Malvolio's entrance in Act 2, Scene 3, the cacophonous singing and drunken revelry is contrasted with the sober appearance of the steward. Likewise, Sir Toby's insulting 'Sneck up' causes hilarity, making the audience laugh at Malvolio's pomposity being punctured. Yet there are more discordant aspects which prevent us from seeing this as 'light-hearted': Sir Toby seems to have a darker aspect to his unruliness, using his status to remind Malvolio of his subordinate status when he asks 'Art thou any more than a steward?' The troubling aspects of misrule in the play seem biting rather than light-hearted.

As you read the student responses, you will have noticed both are written in clear English and show understanding of the play and its events. But you will hopefully have noticed that the second response is better.

Re-read the responses in conjunction with the following commentaries:

Sample answer 1 doesn't really focus on the key debate. The student has overlooked the central comedic aspect in the question – misrule – and chosen an example of humour to write about that really has nothing to do with misrule. Once this error has occurred, it becomes difficult for the student to show their abilities, and difficult to reward the answer. There is an attempt to look at humour, however: the basic idea that laughter arises in Orsino's mistaking of Viola. Once again, though, the student adopts a loose approach to the key terms and interprets 'light-hearted' and 'hilarious' in a general way as 'funny', rather than as more specific terms. There is some sense that this is a drama with an audience but no real grasp of Shakespeare's method. Quotations are used to illustrate basic points, but the whole response is undermined by the bad choice and inability to see what the question requires.

Sample answer 2 has a much tighter grasp on the task. The focus on misrule is present all the way through and the student chooses a sensible part of the play to explore this question. Some thoughtful points around 'hilarious' are offered, with the convincing example of Malvolio's entrance being well used to illustrate this. There is a sense that the dramatic qualities of the play are brought out and the wider comedic ideas such as pomposity are being considered. There is an equally good focus on 'light-hearted' and the student uses this to introduce a thoughtful counter-argument that the comedy has darker elements. Quotations aren't extensive but are judiciously chosen and the phrasing is fluent. The strength of this response is that it approaches the debate head-on and organizes the answer around the key terms in the task.

Activity 3

Write your own paragraph to answer the task you explored in Activity 2. Choose different examples from those used in Sample answer 2 to support your view.

Planning and structuring an answer

At A/AS level, planning and thinking before you write becomes even more important. A coherent, well-structured response does not happen unless some degree of forethought occurs. As you saw above, focusing closely upon the key terms and structuring an answer around them is the key. Once you've identified the point of the task, it makes sense to follow the six steps on page 108.

1. Think carefully about the whole narrative of the play. Which parts of it – which events and scenes – are going to be most useful in helping you to answer the question? If you are engaging with a debate, are there parts of the play that show the character or theme in different lights?

2. Jot down a list of points you wish to make, ensuring that each one relates to the question. Resist any temptation to show off knowledge that isn't relevant to the question.

3. Choose some quotations to include in the body of the essay.

4. Work out a 'route through' your essay. It may well be that in a debate-style task, you will want to start by looking at the main view proposed in the task, and then move on to alternative views.

5. Work out what your conclusion will be. Your conclusion needs to be a strong statement that gives your definitive answer to the question. The best writing is often committed to a certain view, but acknowledges the contrasting or conflicting elements of the debate.

6. Use your conclusion to help you write your introduction.

Writing convincing introductions

A good introduction should signpost an argument. Ideally, the person who reads your work should be able to get a sense of what your argument is going to be. If you plan your answer properly and know what your conclusion will be, then you can signal it in your introduction.

Activity 4

Compare the following two introductions. Which is the more effective, and why?

> How far do you agree that Shakespeare presents misrule as a light-hearted and hilarious aspect of *Twelfth Night*?

Student A

When Shakespeare wrote 'Twelfth Night', he'd already produced several comedies and in the play he employs many story events that appeared in earlier plays. There are original parts of the plot, though, and also some imaginative scenes where the humour really comes to the fore. The audience is treated to a downbeat opening scene but, by the middle of Act I, funnier actions are shown. Some of the comedy is based on misunderstanding and some is based on misrule.

Student B

> The comedic genre often relies upon misrule – the deliberate overturning
> of accepted custom – to provoke laughter. Very often, the inversion of
> power structures leads to hilarious moments where authority is mocked and
> characters of lesser status enjoy power. There is also a sense of danger around
> these moments, though, and, while misrule can be comic, it's difficult to see it
> as a light-hearted aspect of the play. Instead, we see misrule as a double-edged
> sword, provoking hilarity but also flirting with cruelty.

Choosing quotations

One of the arts you need to master is that of selection. In a play containing many memorable lines, being able to select the most relevant quotation to help you make a point is essential. Quotations can be just a few words in length, but should be judiciously chosen. Lengthy quotations often get in the way of a good point. Embed short quotations within the body of your paragraphs, using them as ways to sum up a point or as a springboard to move on.

Activity 5

a) Re-read Act 2, Scene 3. If you were required to answer the task below which lines or phrases from this scene would you select to support or challenge the view given? What would your arguments be?

> How far do you agree that Shakespeare presents misrule as a light-hearted and hilarious aspect of *Twelfth Night*?

b) Using the skills you have practised so far, plan an answer to this task. You should:

1. Select the most relevant parts of the text to write about.

2. Work out what your argument will be.

3. Select useful quotations.

4. Make a list of the points you will make, in order.

Now write a full answer to this task following your plan.

Sample questions

1 To what extent do you agree with the view that Orsino is a character the audience never warms to?

2 Explore how power is presented in the play, paying close attention to the social status of the characters.

3 Would you agree that *Twelfth Night* is a 'miserable excuse for a comedy'?

4 Consider the role and function of Malvolio in the play. Would you agree he is impossible to sympathize with?

5 Explore the role of Olivia in Act 3, Scene 4. Does the rest of the play confirm that she is a victim of love's plague?

6 Explore the presentation of unrequited love in Act 1, Scene 1. Is it true that in the rest of the play unrequited passions lead to despair?

Sample answers

Sample answer 1

> To what extent do you agree that Shakespeare presents cruelty as a major contributing factor to the humour of *Twelfth Night*?

A direct opening which, although lacking subtlety, gives a view.

There are many examples of cruelty in *Twelfth Night*, especially in the scenes involving Malvolio, so it is true that a lot of the humour in the play happens because of moments where characters are cruel towards each other. One of the examples I will talk about is the trick played on Malvolio.

This segment spends too much time re-telling the story rather than building an argument or analysing.

This comes about because Malvolio has told Sir Toby and the others to be quiet in Olivia's house or 'take leave of her'. Maria then hatches a plan to write a letter, pretending to be from Olivia, telling her steward to smile and wear yellow stockings.

A straightforward idea that needs more thought and justification.

This is funny but it is quite cruel because Malvolio seems happy when he believes that Olivia is attracted to him. Therefore cruelty is part of the humour.

The text detail is a bit hazy here and slightly inaccurate.

Another example of cruelty is when Feste teases Malvolio and locks him in a dark room. All of the characters try to convince Malvolio that he is mad even though he isn't.

Another part where the story is being retold; the choice of quotation isn't particularly relevant.

Feste disguises himself as Sir Topas and says 'thou art more puzzled than the Egyptians in their fog'. This is quite funny for the people watching but it's also cruel to Malvolio, so I agree that cruelty is a big part of the humour.

There is a sense here that the characters are real rather than constructs of the playwright.

Malvolio tries to protest his sanity and the audience knows that he is sane and also that he is being tricked, but it's still not a nice trick to play on somebody even though it is funny.

This could be a useful point but there's little depth or exploration.

A third example of cruelty is when Sir Toby arranges a fight between Sir Andrew and Viola. Although he is his friend, Sir Toby is cruel to him and makes him scared just for a laugh.

I think this part is funny, but I agree that it's cruel too. Sir Toby gets attacked by Sebastian at the end, which he deserves. Maybe the worst example of cruelty is when Malvolio is publicly humiliated in the last scene.

Another good idea which goes unexplored.

This response operates at a simple level. There is some focus on the debate, but no depth to the argument. For the most part, the characters are written about as if they are real people. There is little awareness of Shakespeare as the constructor of the text, and no links made to genre or other context. The writing style, while clear, lacks flair.

Sample answer 2

> To what extent do you agree that Shakespeare presents cruelty as a major contributing factor to the humour of *Twelfth Night*?

Comedy as a genre can appear inconsequential, causing laughter without any serious element, yet this is not the case in *Twelfth Night*, where the audience is asked to decide not only whether cruelty meted out to characters is funny, but also whether it produces an uncomfortable type of laughter. Undoubtedly, cruel actions are perpetrated in the play, yet there are other forms of comedic behaviour that do not have their roots in cruelty, but provoke mirth nonetheless. Whether cruelty is the dominant force behind the humour is debatable: it is often the case that wordplay, slapstick and other forms of comedy generate humour too.

This opening successfully places the play (and the debate set up in the question) firmly against the backdrop of the genre.

This clearly establishes the different ways the task may be argued, signaling a counter-argument.

For instance, there is little cruelty in the wordplay of Feste – the humour relies upon distorting meanings and exploiting the multiple meanings of words. His punning conversation in Act 3, Scene 1 with Olivia, where he claims to 'live by the church' is witty rather than cruel. Likewise, upon his first entrance in Act 1, Scene 5, his attempt to prove Olivia's foolishness for mourning her brother's passing is witty yet satirical, intended to provoke thought. Whilst Malvolio might think this cruel, the audience rarely does, and often in performance Olivia's manner betrays her affection for the clever, inventive words of her allowed fool.

The student chooses to begin the essay by focusing upon the counter-argument and does a very good job of arguing the case. Sensible, text-linked points are made.

There is also no cruelty in some of the confusions that provide humour in the play. When Sebastian is taken aback in Act 4, Scene 1 upon meeting Olivia (she thinks he's Viola) and remarks bemusedly, 'What relish is this?', the effect is light-hearted humour. Some of Sir Andrew's misinterpretations (for example, his 'Good Mistress Accost' in Act 1, Scene 3) and the dancing and silly songs of Act 2, Scene 3 contain no discernible element of cruelty.

This paragraph extends the counter-argument, choosing a different form of comedy to make its point.

Yet, undeniably, cruel actions abound in the play, some of which lead to laughter: comedy often requires a comic butt, and the laughter directed towards the target of a joke can be cruel in nature. This is certainly true of the plot against Malvolio, in which his public humiliation is held up for the amusement of the on-stage characters and the audience too.

Once more, the wider genre and its conventions are used effectively, this time to lead into the student's main argument.

When Maria observes 'you have not seen such a thing as 'tis' in Act 3, Scene 5 there is utter glee in the dramatic spectacle of a yellow-stockinged, grotesquely smiling Malvolio, a feeling shared by the other plotters.

A very good point is made about Shakespeare's method and its effect, all linked to the task. There is a good sense of the play as a dramatic construct.

In Act 3, Scene 4 where the deluded Malvolio appears on stage, his humiliation is complete. Here Shakespeare's use of dramatic irony helps bring out the comedy and indeed the cruelty inherent in the scene: the audience is in on the joke too, and it's only the hapless steward who doesn't understand his folly.

Here a convincing personal view in a refined view of the debate is offered, all the while tethering the point to comedic issues.

At this point in the play, it could be said that the comedy stays on the right side of mockery; after all, Malvolio's comeuppance seems justified given his curmudgeonly manner. Yet in the dark room scene, for some audience members the line between comic mockery and simple cruelty is crossed. Dramatically, this can often be an uncomfortable scene, depending upon how the director chooses to stage it, but often the incarceration and Malvolio's pleading tip the balance. Here I would argue that there is cruelty, but actually it is also funny, albeit uncomfortably so. Shakespeare structures this strand of the narrative – Malvolio's humiliation – so the audience enjoy the initial humour, but are then challenged to decide for themselves not only whether the steward's treatment is cruel, but whether it is actually humorous at all. For me, it is both cruel and funny: comedy requires at times a darker edge to take it beyond the simple, light-hearted action of much comedic drama. Without the Malvolio plot and its cruel machinations, the play would lose the balance between light and shade that defines the play.

The final point is perceptive and links to the wider significance of the play.

Overall, this response is highly effective: it focuses on the task very closely and the argument feels convincing. References are used well and there is a good awareness of method. The personal voice comes through in the writing, which is committed and fluently written. Links to the genre are effective.

Activity 6

Compare your essay from Activity 5 to the sample student responses on pages 111–113. Is it more like Answer 1 or Answer 2? How might you set about improving your response?

Writing about extracts

There will be times when you are required to write in detail about a scene or a section of the text, so it is important that you are aware of the skills you need to practise if you write a close analysis of a specified part of the play.

Unlike a traditional essay, an extract task directs you to a specific moment in the play as the place to begin your answer. Yet it is essential that you look closely at the accompanying task because you are unlikely to be asked to write a running commentary on the extract. Instead, a debate or opinion is likely to be offered, and your job is to use the extract as a starting point to explore that debate or opinion. Extract tasks invariably require you to broaden your answer to include the rest of the play, and make links between the content of the extract and what happens elsewhere in the story.

When you are presented with an extract, you might ask yourself the following questions before you begin to frame an answer:

- Identify where in the play the extract comes from. What has happened in the previous scene? What happens in the next scene?
- What is happening in the extract? What is the plot outline?
- Which characters appear in the extract? Who has most lines? Are any characters on stage but silent?
- Where is the scene set?
- Is this a scene where action is important or is it a 'quiet' scene where the reflections of the characters are more important?
- How does the extract commence? Is there anything significant about the first line?
- How does the extract end? Is there anything significant about the last line?
- How is dialogue used? Is there a soliloquy?
- What major themes are explored in the extract?
- Does this extract introduce a new character or theme?
- Are earlier events echoed in the extract?
- Does the extract have any bearing on the end of the play?
- Does this extract change your mind about any of the characters?

Once you have made notes on the general direction and point of the extract, turn your attention to the task. As ever, identify the debate or opinion at the heart of the task. Here are some specific things you could do:

- Underline the key terms in the task and make concrete links between the terms and the content of the extract.

- Re-read the extract, highlighting key pieces of dialogue or quotations that link with the task.

- Begin to frame your argument, making a list of clear points you will make in your answer.

- Consider the rest of the play and how it links to the extract in terms of character or theme. Select parts of the play or quotations that will illuminate your answer, or ones that might provide you with an alternative view.

- Work on your concluding point. What is your central argument/opinion?

Activity 7

Use the following task to help you refine your ability to write about extracts.

> Explore the ways Shakespeare presents love in *Twelfth Night* in Act 1, Scene 4. Would you agree that in the rest of the play, the journey towards love is difficult but happy outcomes emerge?

a) Read the task and extract carefully, and then plan an answer.

b) Once you have made a plan, draft an introduction and conclusion.

Activity 8

Before you look at a sample response, look closely at your plan and identify your own strengths and areas for development. Use these prompts to help you:

- How closely have I focused on the debate/opinion set up in the task?

- What do I intend to say about method, contexts and genre?

- How much do I plan to say about other parts of the play?

- How fluent and effective is my introduction and conclusion?

Now read the first half of a sample response on pages 116–117 to the question above, taking note of the points made.

Sample answer 3, first half

> Explore the ways Shakespeare presents love in *Twelfth Night* in Act 1, Scene 4. Would you agree that in the rest of the play, the journey towards love is difficult, but happy outcomes emerge?

The play explores different facets of love and, in Act 1, Scene 4, the dominant idea seems to be that love causes problems. In Act 1, Scene 4, the comedic problems are still in the throes of being established: we already know that Orsino has unrequited feelings for Olivia but, by the end of this scene, the audience discovers that Viola is in love with Orsino.

When the scene opens, the dialogue between Valentine and Viola prior to Orsino's entrance allows the audience to see that the disguised heroine is testing the water. Her enquiry 'Is he inconstant, sir, in his favours?' gets straight to the heart of lovers' fears – Can I trust this person? Here, Shakespeare arranges the scene so that, upon later readings, we realize that he is inconstant, despite Valentine's claims – he quickly exchanges Olivia for Viola in Act 5, Scene 1. When read in this way, the play suggests that love, far from being a controllable emotion, is actually beyond the power of human control: so, in a way, faith in love's constancy is misplaced because humans are changeable.

This is a very negative reading of love, but one that chimes with the melancholic view of the world proffered by the play and by the closing song of Feste. Orsino's experiences reinforce this idea: he suffers rejection by Olivia and, in Act 1, Scene 4, directs Viola to try once more. The irony here is that Orsino doesn't really appear to be in love. His feelings, as established in the first scene of the play, are an illusion, but one he firmly believes in. His words have the air of the Petrarchan lover proclaiming the 'passion of my love' and, in performance, his brooding manner can appear studied and hollow. Taken together, the love displayed by Orsino suggests a selfish, narcissistic version of that emotion.

There are hints that the supposed love Orsino feels for Viola in Act 5, Scene 1 is prefigured here. There seems to be a developing intimacy in which the count has 'unclasp'd to thee the book even of my secret soul' and his acknowledgement of Viola's 'boyish' charms can, in some performances, suggest the beginnings of desire. Perhaps the most telling notion of love belongs to the final couplet, delivered in an aside by Viola. Here, love appears to cause pain. The protagonist suffers because she is in love but unable to act upon it. She is put in the painful situation of having to woo on behalf of the man she loves. This 'barful strife' is the overriding image of the early segment of the play: comedy requires obstacles to be overcome in the journey towards happiness and, in Act 1, Scene 4, the central issue is how both Orsino and Viola can find and secure love.

Activity 9

The second part of the task asks you to consider to what extent, in the rest of the play, the journey towards love is difficult but happy outcomes emerge.

Write the second half of this response, looking closely at how the process of love unfolds in the remainder of the play, and whether there is a sense of a happy ending.

Activity 10

Use the following task to help you practise your ability to write about extracts. Read the task and extract carefully, and then write an answer.

> Explore the ways Shakespeare presents Feste in Act 1, Scene 5. Is Feste a playful, sympathetic character in the rest of the play?

Tips for assessment

One of the most important elements of your response is phrasing. As well as taking time to select quotations and build an argument, you should also take time to work on your written expression. At the very least, you need to write with clarity – ensure there are no vague sentences or sections in which your point is obscured by inexact wording.

Reading widely is the best way to improve your phrasing. The more texts you access, the more sentence constructions and individual words you will encounter and adapt for your own purposes. Literary criticism has a certain style, so the more academic writing you read, including journals, study guides, critical magazines and essays, the more you will get a feel for the voice of literary criticism. Broaden your reading by accessing broadsheet newspapers online and reading novels slightly beyond your comfort zone. Listen to spoken radio programmes and engage in discussion with other students when possible. Above all, craft your writing. Draft and redraft your phrasing until it conveys precisely what you want it to say.

Glossary

agent of resolution a force, event or character that helps to bring about an end to the problem(s) in the story

allowed fool a jester or fool who is permitted to make entertaining, yet often truthfully critical, comments

alter ego a person's second identity

antagonist a character, often a villain, who acts as an obstacle in the narrative

anti-Petrarchan an attitude in some writing that deliberately presents a lover in 'realistic' rather than idealized ways

apostrophe a direct address to a third party, sometimes an inanimate object

archetype a typical example; the original pattern or model of something

aside lines spoken directly by a character to the audience, which other onstage characters don't hear

aural image image that appeals to the sense of hearing

backstory events that have happened before the play begins

bawdy humour jokes based on sex and risqué matters

blazon originally a coat of arms or a shield on which pictures representing the family were depicted; by extension, a poem that provides a list of the attributes of a lover

caricatured made fun of through exaggerating the appearance or manner of someone or something

carpe diem a latin term meaning 'seize the day' and, by extension, a poem or text type in which a would-be lover urges his mistress to make the most of time

catalyst in literary terms, a character or event that brings about change in others

character arc the progress and development of a character during the text

choric performing the role of chorus, a term derived from Greek tragedy where a group of actors standing aside from the action of the play offer collective comment on events

cliché a phrase so overused and familiar that it appears stale

climax the high point of a narrative

comedic problem the obstacle or issue that has to be overcome in order for the characters to find love or happiness

complication an event that intensifies an existing conflict

couplet two consecutive lines which rhyme

dialogue the words spoken between characters

double entendre a phrase with a double meaning, often a risqué one

dramatic comedy an amusing play that tells the story of how characters overcome problems and find happiness

dramatic irony where the audience possesses more knowledge than the characters about events unfolding on stage

essentialist criticism looking for the essence of a character itself, as if the character had a 'real' existence

exclamatory an often dramatic phrase ending with an exclamation mark

farce comedy based on the pursuit of love, sex or money; it includes fast-paced absurd events

hyperbole a type of exaggeration

imagery the use of visual or other vivid language to convey ideas

imperative a command or order

ironic where a secondary meaning is implied, often one that reveals the truth of a situation

metaphor a comparison between entities implying that one thing is another

metatheatrical where a play contains lines or events that draw attention to its own play-like qualities

mockery making fun of something or someone, drawing attention to aspects of their behaviour that seem odd or amusing

oxymoron a figure of speech that combines contradictory words or images

parody an imitation of a person or genre for comic purposes

pathos the feeling of pity or sadness

phallic symbol an object that represents or symbolizes the penis

physical comedy where humour arises from movement and manner

postcolonial an approach to interpreting a text which looks at issues of power and control in those cultures affected by colonization; also, a text type – one set in countries that experienced colonization and its aftermath

protagonist a central character in a text, often a heroic figure

pun a play on words; a double meaning

representational criticism seeing characters and situations as constructs – versions of 'real' characters and events; representational readings place emphasis on how they have been shown by the writer and what they reveal about the values of society and the writer

resolution the part of a story where problems are overcome and order is restored

revelation an event in a story where a truth or a secret is discovered

rhetorical devices language techniques that attempt to persuade

romantic heroine the central female character in a text centred on love; a character who overcomes the problems before her

satire humour that pokes fun at people or situations in order to make (relatively) serious points or criticism

schadenfreude the cruel pleasure taken from the downfall of others

simile a comparison between entities using the words 'like' or 'as'

slapstick comedy that relies on comic violence and accidents

soliloquy a speech delivered by a character alone on stage

subplot a second strand to the story, which may be related to the ideas of the main plot

symbolism the use of an object that represents someone or something else

tactile image image that appeals to the sense of touch

trope a metaphorical use of language; from Greek, meaning 'to turn', i.e. where one thing is turned into another

visual image image that appeals to the sense of sight

wit verbal humour that relies on quick thinking and wordplay

OXFORD
UNIVERSITY PRESS

Great Clarendon Street, Oxford, OX2 6DP, United Kingdom

Oxford University Press is a department of the University of Oxford.
It furthers the University's objective of excellence in research,
scholarship, and education by publishing worldwide. Oxford is a
registered trade mark of Oxford University Press in the UK and in
certain other countries

© Oxford University Press 2017

The moral rights of the author have been asserted.

British Library Cataloguing in Publication Data

Data available

ISBN 978-019-841953-2

Kindle edition ISBN 978-019-841957-0

10 9 8 7 6 5 4 3 2 1

Printed in China by Leo Paper Products Ltd

Acknowledgements

Extracts are from William Shakespeare: *Twelfth Night*, Oxford School
Shakespeare edited by Roma Gill (OUP, 2010)

The publisher and author would like to thank the following for
permission to use photographs and other copyright material:

Cover: © Jane Morley/Trevillion Images; **p7:** Photostage; **p10:**
Geraint Lewis/Alamy Stock Photo; **p15, 18:** Photo by Ellie Kurttz
© RSC; **p25:** Photostage; **p28:** Chronicle/Alamy Stock Photo; **p30:**
Photostage; **p31:** Keith Pattison © RSC; **p34:** Geraint Lewis/Alamy
Stock Photo; **p38, 45, 47, 49:** Photo by Ellie Kurttz © RSC; **p53:**
Raffaele De Rosa/Shutterstock; **p58:** Geraint Lewis/Alamy Stock
Photo; **p62:** Photo by Ellie Kurttz © RSC; **p66, 72:** Photostage; **p76:**
Keith Pattison © RSC; **p79:** Richard Dyson/Alamy Stock Photo;
p81: Photostage; **p85:** FremantleMedia Ltd/REX/Shutterstock; **p89:**
Photostage; **p92:** Marc Brenner; **p99:** Fine Line/Renaissance/Kobal/
REX/Shutterstock.

Every effort has been made to contact copyright holders of
material reproduced in this book. Any omissions will be rectified in
subsequent printings if notice is given to the publisher.

We are grateful for permission to reprint extracts from the following
copyright texts:

Cesar L Barber: *Shakespeare's Festive Comedy: a study of dramatic form
and its relation to social custom* (Princeton University Press 2012),
copyright © 1972, reprinted by permission of Princeton University
Press via Copyright Clearance Center.

Alan Bray: 'Homosexuality and the Signs of Male Friendship in
Elizabethan England' *History Workshop Journal* (HWJ) No 29, Spring
1990, reprinted by permission of Oxford University Press Journals
via Copyright Clearance Center.

Larry S Champion: *The Evolution of Shakespeare's Comedy: a study in
Dramatic Perspective* (Harvard University Press, 1970), copyright ©
1970 by the President and Fellows of Harvard College, reprinted by
permission of Harvard University Press.

L Cookson & B Loughrey (Eds.): *Critical Essays on Twelfth Night*
(Longman Literature Guides, 1990), copyright © Longman Group
UK Ltd 1990, extracts from Bill Alexander: '"Why, shall we make
him mad indeed" – directing the "dark Room" scene (Act IV scene
2)'; Susie Campbell: '"The knave counterfeits well – a good knave" –
gender and disguise in *Twelfth Night*'; Kate Flint: 'Carnival and Cruelty
in *Twelfth Night*'; Michael Gearin-Tosh: 'The World of *Twelfth Night*';
Graham Holderness: 'Happy Endgames'; David Lewis: '"What's in
a name?" – games with names in *Twelfth Night*'; Paul Oliver: 'The
Corruption of Language in *Twelfth Night*'; Peter Reynolds: 'Illusion
in Illyria: nothing that is so, is so (IV.4.9)'; and Cedric Watts: 'The
Problem of Malvolio', reprinted by permission of Pearson Education.

Michael Delahoyde: 'Petrarchan Love Conventions', on Washington
State University website, www.public.wsu.edu, reprinted by
permission of the author.

Paul Edmondson: *The Shakespeare Handbooks: Twelfth Night* (Palgrave
Macmillan, 2005), reprinted by permission of the publishers,
Springer Nature.

Keir Elam (Ed): introduction to The Arden Shakespeare: *Twelfth
Night* (Bloomsbury, 2008), copyright © Keir Elam 2008, reprinted
by permission of Bloomsbury Arden Shakespeare, an imprint of
Bloomsbury Publishing Plc.

David Farr: 'The Sea Change' in *Living with Shakespeare: Essays by
Writers, Actors, and Directors* edited by Susanna Carson (Vintage, 2013),
compilation copyright © 2013 by Susanna Carson, reprinted by
permission of Vintage Books, an imprint of the Knopf Doubleday
Publishing Group, a division of Penguin Random House LLC. All
rights reserved.

Penny Gay: *The Cambridge Introduction to Shakespeare's Comedies*
(Cambridge University Press, 2008), reprinted by permission of the
publishers.

D J Palmer (Ed): *Shakespeare: Twelfth Night: A Casebook* (Macmillan,
1972), from Joseph Summers, and from C L Barber, reprinted by
permission of the Palgrave Macmillan, Springer Nature.

Kiernan Ryan: *Shakespeare's Comedies* (Palgrave Macmillan, 2009),
reprinted by permission of the publishers, Springer Nature.

Patrick Swinden: *An Introduction to Shakespeare's Comedies* (Macmillan,
1973), reprinted by permission of the publishers, Springer Nature.

Natasha Tripney: 'Tamsin Greig is resplendent', *The Stage*, 23 Feb
2017, reprinted by permission of the author and The Stage Media
Company Ltd.

Eric Weitz: *The Cambridge Introduction to Comedy* (Cambridge
University Press, 2009, 2014), reprinted by permission of the
publishers.

We have made every effort to trace and contact copyright holders
before publication. If notified, the publisher will rectify any errors
or omissions at the earliest opportunity.